8 KEYS TO
BUILDING YOUR
BEST RELATIONSHIPS

8 Keys to Mental Health Series

Babette Rothschild, Series Editor

The 8 Keys series of books provides consumers with brief, inexpensive, and high-quality self-help books on a variety of topics in mental health. Each volume is written by an expert in the field, someone who is capable of presenting evidence-based information in a concise and clear way. These books stand out by offering consumers cutting-edge, relevant theory in easily digestible portions, written in an accessible style. The tone is respectful of the reader and the messages are immediately applicable. Filled with exercises and practical strategies, these books empower readers to help themselves.

8 KEYS TO
BUILDING YOUR
BEST RELATIONSHIPS

DANIEL A. HUGHES

FOREWORD BY BABETTE ROTHSCHILD

W. W. Norton & Company

New York · London

Copyright © 2013 by Daniel A. Hughes

For information about permission to reproduce selections
from this book, write to Permissions, W. W. Norton & Company, Inc.
500 Fifth Avenue, New York, NY 10110

For information about special discounts for bulk purchases, please contact
W. W. Norton Special Sales at specialsales@wwnorton.com or 800-233-4830

Manufacturing by Courier Westford
Production manager: Leeann Graham

Library of Congress Cataloging-in-Publication Data

Hughes, Daniel A.
8 keys to building your best relationships / Daniel A. Hughes ;
foreword by Babette Rothschild. — First edition.
pages cm. — (8 keys to mental health series)
Includes bibliographical references and index.
ISBN 978-0-393-70820-2 (pbk.)
1. Attachment behavior. 2. Interpersonal relationships.
I. Title. II. Title: Eight keys to building your best relationships.
BF575.A86H84 2013
158.2—dc23
2013027760

ISBN: 978-0-393-70820-2 (pbk.)

W. W. Norton & Company, Inc.
500 Fifth Avenue, New York, N.Y. 10110
www.wwnorton.com

W. W. Norton & Company Ltd.
Castle House, 75/76 Wells Street, London W1T 3QT

1 2 3 4 5 6 7 8 9 0

I wish to dedicate this book to Dan Siegel and his colleagues at the Mindsight Institute, for their creative and comprehensive efforts to enhance healthy relationships.

Contents

Acknowledgments   ix
Foreword by Babette Rothschild   xi
Introduction   xv

KEY 1: Learn Why Attachment Matters   1

KEY 2: Know Your Autobiography and Be Willing to Rewrite It   22

KEY 3: Know Your Brain and Biology   46

KEY 4: Build Your Reflective Capacity   75

KEY 5: Build Your Emotional Competence   91

KEY 6: Master Effective Communication   119

KEY 7: Tinker and Repair   141

KEY 8: Balance Autonomy with Intimacy   155

Index   173

Acknowledgments

I have been fortunate over the years to have had many, many wonderful relationships with many people who are very special to me. I must begin with my parents, Marie Collier and William Hughes, who provided me with the knowledge that I was loved and always would be. Alongside was my maternal grandmother, Mary Meehan, who lived with us and who always seemed to have time for me when I wanted her time. And I also must include my six siblings, with whom I learned about laughter and anger, sharing and not sharing, giving and receiving. I continue to learn from them to this day. I would never have written this book without the presence in my life, beginning when I was 17 years old, of Rev. Edward Murray, who was a mentor and guide in my journey from adolescence well into adulthood.

I cannot mention one friend without mentioning many. There have been many moments of joy and sadness, accomplishing tasks and having fun and adventure together, remember the past, enjoying the present and planning the future. Finally, I think of my children and my grandchild. I have received from them at least as much as I have given to them. My life story is as much about being a father and grandfather as it is anything else.

What accomplishments I have attained in my life are not mine. They reflect what I have received from these many special people who are part of who I am. This book would not have been written without the inspiration that I have received for a number of years from Dan Siegel and the Mindsight Institute. Using the current extensive research about the workings of the brain, Dan and colleagues have demonstrated how much the functionality of our brains depends on having healthy relationships—that brains are, in fact, designed to maintain relationships. The Mindsight Institute is committed to spreading the word about this symbiotic relationship between relationships and the brain, and to facilitating the development of relationships among individuals, groups, communities, and nations.

And finally a note of gratitude to Andrea Costella Dawson, who has been my most creative and patient editor for all of my books with Norton, to the other excellent professionals at Norton, and to Babette Rothschild.

Foreword

Babette Rothschild, Series Editor

Humans are social animals. Our relationships are woven in, around, and through the fabric of our beings and are entwined in everything we do. We need them for our survival, which is why humans band together in tribes, fellowships, communities, and countries. We attach to other humans, to animals, even to *stuffed* animals. Most of us need to live in proximity to and in relationship with others. Even when we find ourselves alone, we find *something* to connect with.

A poignant example is illustrated by Tom Hanks in the 2000 movie *Cast Away*. After a plane crash, Hanks's character finds himself stranded and completely alone on an uninhabited island, with not even a monkey or mouse to nurture or relate to. In desperation he eventually develops an attachment to a volleyball that turns up on the beach with him. He draws a face on the ball and calls it "Wilson." In a particularly desperate and touching scene, Hanks's character loses Wilson while trying to escape the island on a raft. The importance of his relationship to the ball is reflected in his desperate cries as he nearly drowns trying to recover it.

Long story short, we need others. We've known this for a long time through intuition and common sense, but now neuroscience research confirms the human (and primate) need for relationships. The discovery of mirror neurons in the mid-1990s is still heralded for underscoring our need for attachment. Mirror neurons form the foundation of our empathy and insight, make it possible for us to connect to another person, to recognize their movement and feel their emotions. Moreover, studies have shown that in disorders such as autism and Asperger's Syndrome, which are often characterized by a deficit in social skills and relationship building, the mirror neuron system does not function properly. If we lived alone—each our own island—a mirror neuron system would be useless. Its very existence is neurological evidence of the human need to build relationships.

A primary goal of the 8 Keys to Mental Health Series is to provide accessible information and practical tools on a range of psychology topics that can help improve the human condition. Because relationships are so important to all of us, a book on the subject has been a priority of this series. Dan Hughes was my first choice to write it. He happened to be a trainer at Family Futures—an organization in London that helps protect children from abuse and neglect—where I was also a periodic lecturer. Over the course of several years I heard about Dan and his work from people who were applying his theories and techniques to their work with children and families. They could not say enough good things about the usefulness of his work and about the man himself. What a delightful coincidence to discover that he was already a successful and well-respected author with W.W. Norton. Voilà! The perfect match of author, publisher, and series.

For over 20 years, Dan has specialized in helping children, couples, and families establish and maintain secure relationships. As an attachment therapist and author of numerous books on the subject, he is, in essence, a relationship expert.

8 Keys to Building Your Best Relationships takes the paradigm of attachment theory, which is what professionals understand to be the driving force behind our ability—or inability— to connect to others, and distills it down to 8 "key" guidelines that we can all easily understand and follow. The book is packed with clinical wisdom, insightful theory made simple and accessible, illuminating stories, and constructive exercises. On each page, readers will be guided to better understand both themselves and the people closest to them. Through this understanding, and with application of the 8 keys, you will be helped to build relationships that are satisfying and lasting.

Introduction

Who are you? Such an important question. One asked over the centuries by poets and philosophers, ministers and politicians. And most likely at times by you and your partner. Why does this question serve as the starting point for this book, a book on relationships? Shouldn't a book on relationships focus instead on the techniques of building a relationship? Shouldn't such a book begin with the question, What is a relationship?

When you ask, Who am I? in part you are asking what sort of relationship you seek and are comfortable with. In coming to know who you are, you can learn how you approach and maintain your relationships. New relationships, if they are important to you, will be influenced by who you were and they will, in turn, influence who you will become.

One of the most important theories about the characteristics, development, and stability of relationships is what is known by professional psychologists and developmental specialists as *attachment theory*. Attachment theory says that infants instinctively turn to their caregivers for safety (food, warmth, protection from frightening things) and for interactions involving eye contact, nonverbal communication, and touch. Indeed, people of all ages turn toward their attachment figures (parents, partners, mentors, best friends) for comfort, support, and companionship. The response we receive from our attachment figures—consistently warm and welcoming or irregular and distant—determines whether we're securely or insecurely attached. And being insecurely attached can sometimes make it challenging to forge healthy relationships. An adult who is securely attached—an adult who is independent and confident enough to have healthy relationships—has a coherent, well-organized life story (what professionals call an "autobiographical narrative"). And so, your life story—your sense of yourself over time, from cradle to grave —can be written by describing the nature of your important relationships.

So, if you decide to continue reading this book, you will—hopefully—have a better understanding of who you are, especially when it comes to the nature of your relationships. You will notice qualities of yourself that influence the initiation, development, and stability of your relationships. You will also notice qualities of yourself that enable relationships themselves to influence—or fail to influence—you and your development. For if relationships are to be healthy, that is, if they are to bring a richness, variety, energy, and wisdom to your life that would otherwise not be present, they will influence you and your development. Identifying how your relationships influence you, and how you, in turn, influence your relationships, is key to building relationships that are stronger, more fulfilling, and longer lasting.

So, again, who are you? This book addresses many features of who you are—your relationship history, the nature and functioning of your brain, features of how you think and feel, how you communicate, with words and without words, how your relationships go wrong and what makes them go right. And finally, this book will help to enhance your own well-being while fostering the well-being of your important relationships.

8 KEYS TO
BUILDING YOUR
BEST RELATIONSHIPS

KEY 1

LEARN WHY
ATTACHMENT MATTERS

Stephanie found that she was very attracted to Jonathan, so much so that she was thinking about giving up a satisfying position at her firm in order to move with him to another city where he had been transferred. She was worried because she did not know him very well. She was even more worried because in the past 8 years she had greatly disrupted her life twice in similar situations in her efforts to have a relationship with a man, efforts that proved unsuccessful both times. Yet Stephanie knew that no matter what she told herself about the need for caution, she was likely to give everything up once again. She wanted to listen to a friend of hers telling her that she needed to go slow, but she found herself impulsively saying yes to Jonathan's suggestion that she move away with him, away from her deeply satisfying career and her community. To better understand Stephanie's behavior, it helps to understand a bit about attachment theory.

Are you comfortable turning to your partner for comfort or guidance? Do you lean on your best friend for support when you experience distress? How do you handle conflict with your partner or friend and how do you repair your relationship after conflicts arise? These questions get at the heart of identifying what makes a relationship healthy, and their answers can be found within attachment theory.

Attachment Theory

Attachment theory emerged in London, England, around 1950 as a model for understanding central features in an infant's relationship with his or her parents. The concept was developed by John Bowlby, an English psychiatrist. The theory—with the active collaboration of Mary Ainsworth—quickly gained traction in the United States, incorporating a strong research component. It has gradually evolved into a central organizing theory worldwide to explain how human beings develop in the context of relationships at all ages. Attachment theory delineates how infants' early relationships with their parents influence the central characteristics of all future relationships. This theory has come to describe key features of these relationships, features that are present among all types of relationships across many cultures and situations.

Attachment theory helps us to understand not only meaningful relationships—both healthy and not so healthy—but also how the person within the relationship functions. Because of our attachment histories, we tend to approach relationships with patterns of thought, emotion, and behavior that are relatively consistent over time and between relationships. The realities of our attachment patterns permeate the way we relate, as well as the nature of our relationships.

In addition, how we are perceived by our attachment figures greatly influences our self-perception. Attachment relationships influence who we are much more than do relationships in which we don't feel particularly attached to the other person.

As all this makes clear, in understanding healthy relationships, attachment matters. In this chapter I will present an overview of attachment and its central characteristics. This will help to create a scaffold as I explore the remaining seven keys to a healthy relationship in the rest of this book. Qualities inherent in attachment theory will be made evident as I describe the features of healthy relationships and outline ways of attaining them.

The Infant's Attachment: From Safety and Security to Exploration

Attachment begins with safety. When infants are in distress—when they experience a threat to their safety—their parents meet their needs, whether for food, warmth, comfort, or engagement, and these infants' distress is relieved and they are ready to be engaged with the next moment in their day. For an infant, attachment is necessary for survival because the infant is not able to meet his or her own most basic needs. Infants need their parents.

Safety

Intellectually, you certainly know that you needed your parents when you were very young, but do you recall any specific instances when you felt a need of them? Do you recall times when you were hurt or frightened? Did you seek out your parents or did they come to you when you cried? Most likely, both patterns generally occurred: You sought their help and they came to you when you were in distress. If, however, for whatever reason, they did not provide help when you needed it, you may have developed a habit of not seeking help from others when you are in distress. In fact, when hospitalized infants undergoing medical procedures experience intense, ongoing pain that their parents are not able to reduce, those infants are at risk for reducing their readiness to turn to their parents in the future when in distress.

As infants experience their parents' keeping them safe again and again in situations involving all manner of threats, they begin to feel increasingly secure within their relationships with their parents. They expect that their parents will keep them safe, and they do. They come to notice that their parents are different from other adults in many ways—primarily involving the parents' consistent ongoing contact with the infants and their being ready and able to keep them safe. The infants increasingly recognize that their sense of security relates to being near their parents and interacting with them. The infants develop a strong desire to be with their parents rather than with other adults. They are likely to develop various degrees of anxiety when other adults are present but their parents are not. They are secure when they are with their parents. They can trust their parents' ability and motivation to care for their needs.

You might recall, when you were a young child, experiencing anxiety when you encountered a stranger. If you were a shy child your anxiety is likely to have been more intense and pervasive that that of a more assertive child. If your parents were sensitive and responsive to your anxiety, supporting you while assisting you in making small steps toward managing your anxiety so that you might engage other adults more easily in the years ahead, it is probable that you will have developed rather good social skills in your relationships with peers and strangers. If you experienced frequent separations from your parents or if they did not support you in your efforts to develop social skills, then there is a good probability that you do not feel safe in novel or stimulating social situations.

Through countless interactions with their parents, infants discover that their parents are an intrinsic part of their life. While parents may be absent for periods of time, infants can count on them to return. The continuity of the relationship gradually becomes expected and the child is secure in knowing that separations or differences come and go but the relationship endures. The young child intuitively knows how to strike a balance between the assurance of safety while beginning to explore the world. The young toddler often will crawl away from the parent, only to crawl back quickly at the first hint of something that seems frightening or when the child becomes uncomfortable with the length of the separation. When the young child is able to successfully manage the balance between safety and exploration, he or she is considered to be securely attached with his or her parents.

Exploration

When infants and toddlers feel safe, and when they trust that their parents are available and willing to protect them in the face of future distress, their security of attachment enables them to focus their abundant energies on exploring the world. When infants are secure, they are in a position to seek to learn about the world. With security comes the endless curiosity that so characterizes the open and engaged psychological state of the young child. This drive to explore is crucial to the child's psychological, physical, neurological, emotional, and behavioral development. Thus attachment security underlies the child's comprehensive development, which goes far beyond the features of attachment.

What is the infant most interested in exploring? Mozart, mobiles, *Sesame Street*? Not so much. Infants and young children are most interested in exploring the worlds of their parents' experience. They are fascinated by what their parents are fascinated by. And their parents are fascinated by *their child*! When parents experience and express joy, delight, love, and interest when they are engaged with their child, the child in turn experiences him- or herself as being joyful, delightful, lovable, and interesting. Beyond this, the meanings that the child places on the objects and events of his or her world are the meanings that the child's parents give to those features of the world.

It was my first night in Australia, and I was unsuccessfully trying to sleep through my jet lag when I noticed two moving shadows on the ceiling. Turning on the light I saw two giant spiders. Much activity followed and I slept very little that night. The following day, in telling some friends about my experience, I discovered that the intruders were known as huntsman spiders. As I told my tale of terror, I noticed that my friends' two sons, ages 8 and 5, had begun listening. The 8-year-old, puzzled by my fear, asked, "Was it just a huntsman?" "*Just* a huntsman!" I exclaimed. The 5-year-old did not understand at all what I was upset about and when his brother explained to him that I was afraid of a "huntsman," he dissolved in laughter. Where did these little boys find their courage?

There was no courage involved. These children had simply learned that in the world of their parents—and seemingly the majority of people in Australia—what they familiarly called the huntsman was not to be feared. Maybe they see them in a way similar to how we see hamsters. The point that I'm making is that parents influence how we see the world through thousands of interactions that we have with them. Most of these are not "instructional." Our parents have a major influence on how we perceive, think about, and act within the world, especially the world of relationships.

When infants are securely attached to their parents, the process of learning about themselves from their parents, and the world, is much more comprehensive, complex, and organized than it would be if their attachments were insecure. Within an insecure attachment their abilities would revolve around trying to attain a sense of safety. Insecure infants are less likely to notice things that don't concern security. A relationship that is characterized by insecurity is likely to lack the range and depth of shared experiences that are common in relationships in which the child is securely attached. Within insecure attachments, a child is apt to learn much less from his or her parents and, at the same time, to learn much less about him- or herself and the world generally.

To apply the concept of infant attachment to the realm of adulthood, when we are secure in a relationship, knowing that it will persist even in the face of problems and that we are able to turn to the other when we are in distress, we are more open to learning about all sorts of things when we are in the presence of the other. When we travel with someone to whom we are securely attached, we tend to be more relaxed, to enjoy our travels more, and to be more open to learning from new experiences than if we traveled alone.

Your Blueprint for Relationships

At the same time as infants are developing an attachment to their parents, they are developing a blueprint for how to engage with others with whom they have meaningful bonds. This blueprint serves as a guide for the following:

- How we communicate and our perceptions, expectations, and general manner of relating with other members of our family or close friends. Attachment researchers call this an *inner working model* for how relationships work, what can be expected from them, and what role to give them in our lives.
- How much we are likely to rely on others and the areas in which we do rely on them.
- The role of emotions in our relationships—how direct and expressive we are, how vulnerable we are willing to be, and how much we rely on emotions to determine the nature and importance of a given relationship.
- How easy it is for us to trust another person to be available when we are in distress and to remain committed to us in spite of differences or conflicts.

This blueprint for how we relate to others is not rigid and impermeable to change. However, it does provide us with a pattern of relating to others that is consistent over time and across relationships. This pattern influences the role that we give relationships in meeting our need for safety, as well as the role of relationships in our learning about the world.

Patterns of Relating

Attachment researchers have determined that individuals tend to fall into one of three primary relationship patterns; a fourth overlaps these three patterns. Researchers have given one name to each of these patterns when it applies to children and another when it applies to adults, as shown in the table. For example, a child who demonstrates an *ambivalent* pattern of attachment would display a *preoccupied* pattern on reaching adulthood (assuming that this individual's pattern has not changed in the meantime as a result of significant life experiences and new relationships).

Being aware of which pattern we tend to demonstrate in our relationships can help us understand our preferences, emotional-behavioral habits, and relationship challenges. As noted earlier, these patterns are not rigid. They tend to be stable but can be modified if we work to effect changes through reflection and exploring different ways of relating in existing or new relationships. Let's take a closer look at each of these four attachment patterns in adults. Later in the chapter you'll have the opportunity to figure out which attachment pattern you fall into.

Attachment Classifications	
Childhood	**Adulthood**
Secure	Autonomous
Avoidant	Dismissive
Ambivalent	Preoccupied
Disorganized	Unresolved

The Characteristics of Attachment Patterns

The four classifications of attachment are distinguished by specific approaches to relationships. These approaches are fairly stable and serve as a mental, emotional, and behavioral template for developing and maintaining our important relationships. Below, the elements that signal each constellation of viewpoints and behavior are outlined.

Autonomous Attachment

- You are able to maintain a balance between self-reliance and reliance on a person with whom you are attached.
- Depending on the context, you may choose to manage a situation alone or to manage it with the assistance of your friend or partner.
- You are able to maintain your autonomy while still successfully maintaining continuous relationships with your friends or partner.

Dismissive Attachment

- You tend to diminish the importance of attachment relationships in your life while focusing on protecting your independence and personal control of your life.
- You tend not to think about your attachment relationships much but rather give more value to your personal accomplishments and interests.
- You are likely to deemphasize emotions while stressing your thoughts and reasoning abilities in making life choices and managing stress.

Preoccupied Attachment

- You tend to overemphasize the importance of relationships in your life while deemphasizing the importance of your independence.
- You tend to seek security and happiness within close relationships, but since your sense of your autonomy is not well developed, you tend to be insecure and unhappy in these relationships.
- You tend to dwell on your past relationships a great deal without being able to reduce the influence of those relationships on your present relationships.
- You are likely to deemphasize reasoning while stressing the importance of your emotions in making life choices and managing stress.

Unresolved Attachment

An unresolved attachment pattern is a subset of any one of the preceding patterns. The unresolved attachment pattern emerges when an event within a current attachment relationship reminds you of a similar, very stressful event in a past relationship. This association with the past relationship has a disorganizing, dysregulating effect on your functioning in your current relationship. The unresolved pattern might be present rarely or frequently in one or more of your current relationships. For example, a man may manifest an autonomous (or dismissive or preoccupied) attachment pattern with his partner, but one day when he fails to follow through on a commitment to her and she responds angrily, he may experience his partner as being similar to his mother, who would go into a rage when he lied to her, a rage that caused him to run to his room in terror. This may create, at least temporarily, intense fears of abandonment and shame that make it hard for him to feel safe and repair their relationship.

If you notice a sudden emergence of acute, disruptive, and disorganizing behaviors periodically in your important relationships, these episodes may represent signs of an unresolved attachment. These stressful events and behaviors may continue to reemerge unless you are able to resolve the prior attachment pattern. Such resolution may occur through reflection or through seeking counsel within a personal or professional relationship.

The Importance of Attachment Patterns in Relationships

These attachment patterns suggest that healthy relationships tend to maintain a fruitful balance between connection and autonomy, intimacy and independence. Attaining deep meaning and satisfaction in healthy relationships is much more likely to occur when we also attain satisfaction and joy in solitary and self-initiated activities.

The Larger Context

While the primary model for healthy relationships that is presented in this book is attachment theory, we must remember that issues of gender roles, religion, and culture, as they are expressed within the family and community, are also important in shaping relationships as they develop. Widely held expectations of how boys and girls should develop separately and in relationship with each other certainly influence their relationships throughout life.

Conflicts are certain to occur if a boy is raised to assume that domestic responsibilities are in the realm of women and a girl is raised to assume that both men and women carry out domestic chores in an equitable manner and this boy and girl develop a relationship. The boy so raised may well believe as a man that his female partner does not love him or is being unfair when she expects him to participate in housework. Similarly for the girl: She will not be at ease when she is involved with a male partner who does not do his fair share of domestic chores.

When we consider different expectations in the development of girls and boys, it should not come as a surprise that girls are more likely to develop the preoccupied attachment pattern, emphasizing relationships and emotions, while boys are more likely to develop the dismissive attachment pattern, emphasizing independence and cognition. If both boys and girls are to develop an autonomous attachment pattern, they will need to build intimate relationships while retaining their sense of independence.

Many examples of differing gender expectations exist, involving decision making, taking the initiative, child-rearing, sharing emotions, and being responsible for the health of the relationship, to name some of the more obvious ones. Being aware of such assumptions, discussing them openly, and exploring ways to resolve any significant differences are crucial in maintaining the health of the relationship.

Example

In the following sections I offer contrasting scenarios that describe potential narratives in the case of the development of an individual I call Melanie. The purpose of these scenarios is to demonstrate how attachment relationships have a significant impact on the course of our lives, and that these effects can be modified in various ways, especially through other attachment relationships. While our attachments to our parents greatly influence our development, they are not the only influences, and their effects are not irreversible.

Scenario 1

Melanie was wanted by her parents, Beth and Bruce, from the day she was born. They might have wished that she had waited a few years until they were more settled in their careers and home, but they still embraced her when she arrived. They loved her passionately and took delight in her expressiveness and her apparently endless desire to be held by them and to remain engaged with them. They were not getting much sleep and their quiet weekends of relaxation and finding interesting things to do were long gone, but they found the energy they needed to be parents and to find new sources of pleasure with their daughter.

Over time, the stress of starting their careers and their family, the strain of constant money worries, and the frustration of not being able to find the right day care setting for Melanie after three unsatisfactory attempts left the whole family feeling a bit tense. Melanie began crying more and Bruce and Beth began to find reasons to ask the other to watch her. They still played with her and liked her laughter and curiosity but their interest drifted to other things more quickly and more often. Although they were not aware of it, Melanie became less of a source of delight and more of an obligation. Important to them and loved, yes, but experienced as an obligation nonetheless. And Melanie cried even more and wanted them to hold her more. She wanted them to be the way they were during the first months of her life. Her parents, by contrast, started to want the lives that they had had before she was born.

Nothing that Melanie experienced in early childhood could be regarded as abusive or neglectful behavior. She received her parents' affection. What was missing was more subtle. While children are generally experienced by their parents as both a source of delight and an obligation, Melanie, as the months went on, was too often an obligation and too infrequently a source of delight. She desired more of the emotional intimacy that she sometimes experienced. In striving to attain closer relationships with her parents, she did not devote enough energy toward developing her own independent thoughts and plans. As a child she demonstrated an ambivalent attachment pattern, which led to a preoccupied pattern as she entered adulthood.

Beth and Bruce had grown up in very different families. Beth was the third of five children. Her parents both worked to support the family but eventually came to resent each other, argue a lot, and find their enjoyments outside the family. Beth did not recall having had many enjoyable activities with her mother—with her older sister, yes, but her mother was always working at home and at part-time jobs and just did not have the time to devote to the wishes of each individual child. Her dad had not seen his role as a father as going much beyond putting bread on the table. There was a lot of emotion in Beth's home but too often it was tension and anger. Beth was often "underfoot," seeming to irritate her siblings and parents both with her frequent demands and her dissatisfaction with much of family life. Beth might be described as having been an ambivalently attached child who developed into a preoccupied attached adult. Bruce, by contrast, was the older of two children; his parents were high achievers who invested a lot of energy in their accomplishments and the hoped-for potential future accomplishments of their two children. There was little time for fun among the family members: That was regarded as "wasting time," as Bruce's parents did not want to miss out on any opportunities for advancement. There was little expressed emotion within the home, though his parents were always available and took seriously their role in guiding their children's development. Bruce might be described as having been an avoidant attached child who developed into a dismissive attached adult.

While Bruce and Beth had agreed that they wanted a different kind of family life from those they had known, they found it harder to attain than they anticipated. Their enthusiasm for interacting with their lively infant gradually decreased as they focused on the day-to-day responsibilities of their lives. Beth found herself with most of the child-rearing responsibilities at home, though she and Bruce were both employed outside the home. She became increasingly irritable with Bruce. While she enjoyed caring for Melanie when her daughter responded with interest and laughter, she found it much harder to care for her child when the youngster was cranky and demanding. At times it seemed to Beth that Melanie was rejecting her, and then she would react to her child using a harsh and critical tone. Bruce also enjoyed playing with and caring for Melanie, but for shorter periods of time. He tended to withdraw both from any emotional stress and from expectations from his wife or daughter for extended interactions.

As Melanie grew she revealed her emotional states—her joys and interests and her sadness and fears—less and less to her parents. It's not that she was content to be alone. In fact, she often wanted to be with them rather than play independently. She had more success in becoming engaged with her mother than with her dad, but when she and her mother interacted it often seemed to end in dissatisfaction for both. With her father, Melanie did not try to relate as much. It seemed that he was not that interested and she, too, quickly lost interest as their activities together seemed to lose energy and enjoyment. When her parents directed her toward her peers, she went, reluctantly at first but then willingly. Her peers seemed to respond to her more than her parents did— until they lost interest and had reasons to turn down her invitations to get together. Or she would find them to be unsatisfying. So she looked for other friends and generally was successful in finding them.

As the years went on Melanie seemed to be habitually mildly unhappy. Never anything specific, just mildly unhappy. She had done well at school, was popular and successful at college, and developed a satisfactory career with a small business in the area where she lived. She was well liked at work and sought out friendships, and she generally enjoyed them—for a while. She wanted more from her relationships and more from her activities but she never quite knew what the *more* was. She had frequent relationships with friends and potential partners but they never seemed to last. At times she sensed that she might be too "demanding" in her relationships and too critical of others, but she tended not to think about her part in the relationship failures much. It made her feel too discouraged and a bit ashamed. She knew that her parents loved her and she loved them, but she did not really seem to enjoy her time with them that much. She and her mother tended to squabble about many things, while she and her father had little to say to each other. She was often aware of finding fault with her parents, but again, she did not think about that much because she felt that having such thoughts meant that she was ungrateful.

As she approached 30, Melanie married Arlen, who was quiet and calm and seemed to like her energy and desire for intimacy. She liked how he seemed to just accept her and that he did not pull away when she went out of her way to spend extra time with him. What she had wanted all her life—maybe in hindsight had wanted "too much"—he wanted also. He had wanted such a relationship but had never had the confidence to initiate it. Within a few years they had two adorable young children, a boy and a girl; they loved them with a passion and took immense delight in them. But inevitably the responsibilities mounted, along with the stresses and strain of having many obligations. Arlen became withdrawn and moody and Melanie became tense and unhappy. She tried hard—often with increasing anger and criticism—to have Arlen reengage with her and their children. Arlen began reminding her of her father (no surprise, given that Arlen was showing a dismissive attachment pattern). As the children seemed to want more and more from Melanie each day, she began to feel suffocated by their demands. Something was wrong, but she tried not to think about it because such thoughts left her feeling hopeless. Yet something was also familiar, though she tried not to think about that either. Somehow she sensed that allowing her thoughts to go in that direction might undermine core meanings in her life.

Melanie's story is familiar to us: The relationship patterns of our childhood often return and are evident in the relationship patterns of our adult lives. Or if those patterns do not return, their mirror images appear. These earlier patterns—family patterns involving partners and parent-child relationships—tend to influence the patterns that develop in our new families. But they also make their presence felt in many of our relationships: with friends and colleagues and neighbors and acquaintances. They are present even in the brief functional relationships in which others provide us a service or in which we do so.

Let's revisit the story of Melanie and her parents now, considering two additional scenarios, which describe how her life and attachment patterns might have evolved differently if there had been a few changes in her attachment relationships when she was a child.

Scenario 2

Beth and Bruce experienced passion and delight over their lovely infant daughter. However, as their lives entailed more and more responsibilities, including those of caring for Melanie, they began to experience less pleasure in being her parents and found themselves avoiding spending their free time engaging with her other than handling her basic needs. One evening, after an argument with Bruce over who was "on call" on Saturday afternoon to supervise Melanie, Beth wept and spoke with her husband about her sense that they—and Melanie—were losing something special in their relationships. She recalled with distress noticing herself saying things and reacting to her daughter the way that her parents had reacted to her. Bruce began recalling how much his parents had avoided day-to-day care of him when he was young, and he realized that he was developing the same attitude toward Melanie. They spoke about this quite a bit over the following few weeks and made a commitment to each other to develop new patterns in how they related to their daughter, different from how their parents had related to them.

For months Beth and Bruce supported each other in their efforts to change their way of relating to their daughter. Because of their motivation to be better parents and through mutual support, Beth was able to reduce her preoccupied pattern, while Bruce reduced his dismissive pattern. They each became more autonomously attached and greatly assisted each other in facing their struggles to remain engaged with Melanie in ways that were satisfying to them all. Often Bruce pushed himself to initiate activities with Melanie or to respond to her initiatives when he did not feel like doing so. He worked to convince himself that playing with his daughter was something that was good both for her and for him. Beth pushed herself to experience those things that were positive in her daughter and in their relationship. She let go of small frustrations more easily, developed greater patience, and was less volatile. Gradually Beth and Bruce began to notice that as they interacted with Melanie, they often enjoyed their interactions more over time. This enjoyment emerged more quickly more often. One day, they laughed, with a deep sense of wonder and joy, when they realized that they now were often competing with each other for their daughter's attention, rather than competing to avoid her attention. As Melanie developed, her relationships with her peers were often meaningful, successful, and enjoyable. She eventually chose a partner who also was autonomously attached and they were able to raise their children with a pattern similar to that displayed in how she had been raised by Beth and Bruce.

Scenario 3

Beth and Bruce repeated their parents' pattern in raising Melanie in a manner that contained many of the conflicts and avoidant patterns that characterized how they had been raised. Melanie tended to be unhappy and critical in her relationships with peers and these relationships tended to be short lived.

When she was 12 years old, Melanie happened to develop one such relationship with a girl her age, Jane, who lived a few streets away. She met Jane's family and was invited to join them in some of their family activities and meals. A few months into the relationship, she and Jane had an argument over Jane's not being available to get together with Melanie one weekend. Melanie accused her friend of being mean and selfish. She left, anticipating that she was not likely to see Jane again. The following week, however, Jane called and invited Melanie to go along with Jane and her family to a movie. A few weeks later, Jane's mother scolded Melanie for teasing Jane's brother when Melanie was at their house. Melanie left shortly after that and felt sad that she would not be invited back. But she was in fact invited back—again and again, in spite of conflicts with Jane or Jane's siblings or parents. And the conflicts were fewer and fewer.

Melanie was learning a new pattern of attachment relationships with Jane and her family. Most likely Jane would have been considered to manifest secure attachment, while her parents most likely manifested autonomous attachments. Over the following few years Melanie noticed that her relationships with other peers were lasting longer and had fewer conflicts. She noticed that differences did not lead to anger and anger did not lead to a relationship break. She also noticed that her relationships with teachers tended to be more satisfying. As a young adult, she eventually chose a partner who was autonomously attached and together they were able to raise their children with a pattern similar to what she had learned with Jane and her family and in the subsequent meaningful relationships of her adolescence.

The three scenarios presented for Melanie's developing life are certainly not that clear cut. The failures presented in the first scenario most certainly also contained successes, and the successful changes in her attachment patterns in the second two scenarios most definitely contained stress, mistakes, and discouragement even when the patterns had evolved in a more satisfactory manner. However the dominant attachment patterns described along with their development are each realistic and serve as important principles for understanding the relative strengths and vulnerabilities and satisfactions and troubles inherent in the stories of our lives.

Yes, attachment matters. Our original attachment patterns are blueprints for our lives and we tend to naturally express them in our day-to-day relationships with our current attachment figures and in less important relationships as well. They can be changed, modified, made more flexible and comprehensive. But that is not likely to happen magically when we take a pill, read a book, or enter a new relationship. For these patterns to change and develop in directions that provide more positive meanings and satisfaction, we need to become aware of our patterns, reflect on them, and tinker with personal habits and interactions with others that characterize our relationships. This book can serve as a guide for that challenging and rewarding process.

Exercises

Now that you know the four types of attachment patterns that exist, consider which pattern best describes your behavior. Remember that you may exhibit some features of more than one pattern.

1. Autonomous attachment

   - Are you comfortable handling a problem by yourself *and* relying on someone who is important to you?
   - Are you able to acknowledge the importance of your own interests and wishes as well as the interests and wishes of your partner and to find time for both?
   - Do you value the importance of both your emotional experiences and your more reflective insights?

2. Dismissive attachment

   - Do you focus a great deal on your interests and independence and place less value on relationships?
   - When you plan for the future do your thoughts involve your personal development more than the development of your relationships?
   - Do you adopt a highly rational approach to life's decisions while placing little value on your emotional experiences?

3. Preoccupied attachment

- Do you focus more on your relationships than on your individual interests and pursuits?
- Do you worry a great deal about your important relationships and often find them less satisfying than you wish them to be?
- Does your mind frequently wander to past relationship problems and losses, including those that extend back into childhood?
- Do you find yourself taking action that is driven more by your emotions than by reflection on what the best course might be?

4. Unresolved attachment

- Do you find that certain experiences in your important relationships are extremely difficult to manage?
- Do events from past relationships intrude into your experiences in your present relationships?
- Do you have considerable difficulty regulating your thinking, emotions, and behaviors in certain situations with your partner?

If you think you have features of a *dismissive attachment style* (you tend to deemphasize the importance of relationships and emotions in your life and devalue thinking or talking about them and relying on others at times of stress), ask yourself, and write down your answers to, the following questions:

- What benefits do you think there are in maintaining this style? (What would you not want to give up if you were to change this style and adopt a more autonomous style?)
- What disadvantages do you think there are in maintaining this style? (What would you want to achieve if you were to change this style and adopt a more autonomous style?)
- What initial thoughts do you have about making these changes so as to achieve a more autonomous style? (Revisit this question as you proceed through this book.)

If you think you have features of a *preoccupied attachment style* (you tend to deemphasize the importance of independence and reflection in your life and you tend to have difficulty letting go of relationship stresses from the past and in the present, while not focusing enough on self-reliance during times of stress), ask yourself, and write down your answers to, the following questions:

- What benefits do you think there are in maintaining this style? (What would you not want to give up if you were to change this style and adopt a more autonomous style?)
- What disadvantages do you think there are in maintaining this style? (What would you want to achieve if you were to change this style and adopt a more autonomous style?)
- What initial thoughts do you have about making these changes so as to achieve a more autonomous style? (Revisit this question as you proceed through this book.)

If you think you have features of an *unresolved attachment pattern* that appear at important times in your relationships and if you feel that when under stress you have difficulty successfully relying either on yourself or others (that is, past stressful events continue to adversely affect your functioning in the present), ask yourself, and write down your answers to, the following questions:

- What do you think the past relationship events are that negatively affect your current relationships and functioning?
- What are the effects on your current relationships and functioning?
- What initial thoughts do you have about how to make changes so you can resolve past relationship stresses so they have little or no impact on your current relationships? (Revisit this question as you proceed through this book.)

KNOW YOUR AUTOBIOGRAPHY AND BE WILLING TO REWRITE IT

A book on building healthy relationships has a major chapter focusing on your autobiography? You might wonder if that slants too much toward the introspective for the task we are addressing in this book. You might also assume that because the events of your autobiography, your personal history, have already happened, they are now water under the bridge. You might want to simply look toward tomorrow and focus on strategies that you might use to develop new relationships or to improve the quality of your current relationships. Before skipping to later chapters in the belief that they will be more practical than this one, however, consider several points that will explain why this chapter is included.

First, events that occurred in your past have a major impact on your relationship patterns, and if you want to change these patterns in any way, it is helpful to understand what sorts of effects those past events have had on your perceptions, wishes, and behavior when it comes to your relationships. Second, while past events cannot be changed, it is possible to construct new meanings around them, and if these meanings changed, there is every reason to believe that the impact of the events on your current relationships can change. So go with me into your past for a bit and see if your perceptions of your current relationships and of your desired future relationships change.

Your Autobiography

It is hard to describe to others who you are as a person without mentioning your background and life experiences, including the relationships of your childhood, adolescence, and young adulthood, relationships that so greatly influenced who you are today. Your sense of yourself—your identity—might be characterized as a snapshot of yourself at this moment in the narrative that is your autobiography. Your life story, especially aspects of it that involve the social and emotional world of your relationships, is a central determining factor in who you have become and in large part determines the nature of your meaningful relationships.

Who you are is the result of a unique blend of personal factors: your family of origin, your local community, your culture, your religion or system of beliefs, your nationality and country of residence—your autobiography. This is not to suggest that your temperament, genetic blueprint, and other internal factors are not important. Rather, we are focusing on how the unique patterns and qualities of your past relationships that make up your autobiography have had a major influence on your current relationships. Our lens will focus on your family relationships in particular. Paying attention to relationships with friends and to how your relationships may have been influenced by cultural or religious beliefs, gender roles, customs, and expectations might also be beneficial.

In this exploration of your autobiography, I'm sure you won't be surprised that the central focus will be on your relationships with your parents. The parent-child relationship was your original blueprint for how relationships would develop and be maintained, as well as their characteristics, functions, boundaries, and role in your life. You may grasp how your relationship with your parents had an impact on how you would relate to your children but have greater difficulty seeing its relevance to your relationship with your partner or close friends. There are many ways that your relationship with your parents has influenced the nature of all your important relationships. Before making those connections, let's first explore central features in the parent-child relationship and delve into your unique version of this relationship.

The ten themes discussed below provide a framework for important features in your attachment history, focusing on your relationship with your parents. At the beginning of each section, questions associated with that theme are given. You might find it helpful to write down your responses to these questions as you arrive at each section and then review your responses as you read through this book.

In developing your responses, you may experience emotions associated with various events from your past. These emotions—such as sadness, fear, joy, elation, anger, happiness, shame—are a bridge to the meaning of those events and the impact they have had on who you have become and where you want to go.

Theme 1: Sharing Positive Emotions

Did you and members of your family express love and affection openly with hugs and kisses, words and terms of endearment? Did you share your joys and accomplishments with one another and were these met with pleasure and affirmations in return?

You may want your relationships to be a major source of pleasure and joy in your life. This is more probable if during your childhood there was an ongoing open expression of affection and mutual enjoyment in your interactions with your parents. Children actively seek out and participate in such interactions when they are freely given and received by their parents. If the open expression of positive emotion is lacking, although you may know that you were, and are, loved by your parents, your experience of their love will have been, and remain, less deep. Your awareness of their love is in your head more than in your heart.

If expressions of positive emotion were not a common occurrence in your childhood home, you may be uncomfortable with such expressions in your relationships with your friends or partner. Differences in ways of expressing emotions and levels of being comfortable with such expressions from your partner can become a source of disappointment or frustration in your shared emotional life. There is no right or wrong here. However, an awareness of how important such expressions are to you and your partner and a willingness to openly discuss any differences in how emotions are expressed, and what these differences signify for each of you, may be important components of the health of your relationship.

Theme 2: Sharing Vulnerable Emotions

Did you and members of your family feel comfortable telling one another about fears, disappointments, failures, and unhappiness that were experienced? Was it OK to cry and seek comfort? When you shared your distress, did you receive mostly emotional support or practical advice?

If you were able to reveal your vulnerable emotions to your parents and feel comforted and supported by them in return we can assume that you were securely attached to them. Your freedom to turn to them for comfort and support when you were undergoing emotional distress allowed you to feel their love, and that helped you handle the distressing situation better and maybe even become more resilient in handling other sources of stress. Receiving their comfort and support fostered in you an ability to develop emotional competence that you could use in handling difficult emotions. This allowed you to retain your sense of worth when facing disappointments and failures. You did not have to be perfect or deny mistakes. Learning from ordeals and failures was made easier than it would have been if you had not felt able to seek and receive support from your parents in handling such difficulties.

If you did receive comfort and support from your parents during vulnerable times in childhood, you'll tend to be more comfortable with both giving and receiving such support in your relationship with your partner or good friends. You'll be less likely to believe that you have to go it alone in managing stress. If your friend or partner turns to you for comfort, you'll feel comfortable giving it and, beyond that, pleased to be viewed as someone on whom others can rely for sympathy. If as a child you had been led to believe that seeking comfort was a sign of being weak or dependent—as if dependency in childhood, or at any age, is a fault—you will probably view appeals for comfort from a partner or friend as evidence of weakness and dependency. This could lead to your feeling trapped by your friend's or partner's wish (i.e., demand) for comfort from you and cause you to withdraw from the relationship.

Theme 3: Expressing Anger

Was there a place for anger in your family, both in the general atmosphere and in disputes between individuals? Was there a way to express anger toward your parents or were all expressions of anger thought to be disrespectful? Did your parents usually express anger when they disciplined you? Were your parents often angry at each other, and if so, how was the anger expressed and did it result in a resolution of arguments? If they seldom or never expressed anger toward each other, how do you think that affected their relationship?

Many parents ask and even expect their children to be open and honest with them but do not allow them to express anger toward them. Expressing anger, and, in some families, even acknowledging anger, is seen as a sign of disrespect and provokes a stern verbal response or more serious consequences. When children are exposed to such conditions, many have difficulty identifying, regulating, and communicating anger toward their parents and also toward others. When they express anger toward their peers they often do so in an intense, dysregulated, or aggressive manner. In the parent-child relationship, if there is no place for anger, conflicts are often not managed well—they are either avoided or poorly expressed and not satisfactorily resolved—causing periods of estrangement or sullen irritability. Anger becomes associated with shame, and the reasons for the anger—often vulnerable emotions of sadness, fear, or worry—are not understood, described, and resolved.

If your parents also had difficulty managing and expressing anger toward each other in a way that led toward resolution of the conflict, then you also were not given the experience of seeing adults manage the periodic stresses that are inherent in any intimate relationship.

If anger, then, was not present in your family life, most likely you were not given experience in expressing it toward your peers or siblings in a manner that was not attacking the other person. You were not likely to speak about a challenge in the relationship that you wanted to resolve. Anger may have simply become a way of hurting your friend, being motivated by experiencing hurt yourself in response to his behavior and your perception of what it meant about you and your relationship. If you tend to habitually avoid anger, you are likely to also be leaning toward a dismissive attachment style. If you tend to dwell on angry feelings toward your friend, you are likely to be leaning toward a preoccupied attachment style. If your anger, instead, is a signal to you of a problem that you are experiencing in your relationship, then it is likely to assist you in making sense of the problem, communicating the vulnerable thoughts and feelings that activated the anger, and seeking clarity from your friend and a resolution of the perceived problem. Such a role for anger would serve you well if you were to have an autonomous attachment style.

Theme 4: Resolving Conflicts

After family conflicts, was there any effort to acknowledge the conflict and repair the relationship? Was the conflict dwelled on and reenacted endlessly? Was the conflict denied as if it had never happened? Did conflicts lead to a reduction of the problem or an increase in the problem or did they have no effect on the problem?

If there was a legitimate place for the appropriate expression of anger in your relationship with your parents, it is likely that your family was able to address and resolve the typical conflicts found in all families. When there is a commitment to addressing and resolving conflicts by parents, there are often periods of extended sharing and relaxed mutual enjoyment. By acknowledging and addressing conflicts when they arise, they tend to be milder, last a shorter time, and occur less frequently.

Some parents, following a conflict, are not inclined to talk with the family member with whom they are angry for hours or even days after the conflict. Such parents may not even acknowledge that family member's presence. Such extreme withdrawal from the relationship is likely to elicit shame in most children. The message given by such a retreat is that the behavior of the accused family member—in fact, his or her very person—is so outrageous as to make the person unlovable. Such a response to anger and conflict may be effective in creating compliance in children but it greatly undermines their sense of worth and autonomy, as well as their security in the relationship. The risk of abandonment is not too far away.

If you want to establish and maintain a healthy, long-term relationship with your partner, you would do well to be comfortable with facing conflicts and being committed to resolving them. Honeymoons, those times of overlooking slights and differences and of concentrating on what is best about a partner, never last. In the early weeks and months of your relationship you mostly see those features that attracted you to your partner, creating an image of him or her that overshadows any qualities you might not desire. Eventually those qualities become evident in your relationship and cannot be ignored. If you attempt to ignore them, you will tend to gradually give up spontaneous openness and intimacy in favor of safely getting along. The risk is that in time you might be intimate in name only. If you try to address the conflict but have little experience with appropriate expression of anger while communicating vulnerable emotions and repairing a relationship, you may drift into an endless cycle of conflict, also undermining any deep sense of intimacy.

Theme 5: Expressing Differences

Were variations and differences in thoughts, feelings, intentions, and plans accepted and even encouraged or were they seen as being wrong and unacceptable? Did you believe that you had to keep many of your thoughts and feelings and plans secret, out of fear that your parents would be critical or rejecting?

If differences with your parents during your childhood were neither accepted nor encouraged, and even judged as signs of selfishness on your part, it would have been difficult for you to develop a strong sense of autonomy. Given the narrow range of thoughts, feelings, and behavior that was available to you for organizing your sense of self, you were at risk of possessing only a vague notion of who you were, as a being apart from your parents. The negative judgments from your parents of your inner life will have made it harder for you to know and accept this inner life. As you grew, you learned that you had to choose between your autonomy and your relationship with your parents.

In contrast, if your parents enjoyed and even encouraged the sharing of different interests, opinions, feelings, ideas, and values, you will have gradually come to know the unique qualities that make up the central features of your identity. You will have perceived your relationship with your parents as very important to them and as secure, despite any differences or conflicts. You will have been able to adopt an autonomous attachment style.

Acknowledging and accepting differences in your partner is a central feature in maintaining the health of your relationship. Differences are seen as bringing depth and growth to your relationship rather than being a threat to it. Many relationship problems result directly from efforts by one partner to try to control the inner life—the thoughts, feelings, wishes, and beliefs—and behavior of the other. In such situations, there is an assumption that only one of you can be right; the other must be wrong. Neither partner will accept that the *wrong* category applies to his or her own position.

This wish to control the person with whom you have an attachment—often experienced as a *need* to control—is a central feature in the lives of children who manifest attachment disorganization and with adults who have features of an unresolved attachment style.

Theme 6: Setting Limits and Providing Discipline

Do you recall discipline as being harsh, permissive, or moderate? Did it relate to your behaviors only or also to your thoughts and feelings? Did it consist in relationship withdrawal? Corporal punishment? What were you disciplined for most?

If discipline was harsh and punitive when you were a child and involved frequent outbursts of anger and severe punishments, it is probable that you felt a good deal of fear and shame in your relationship with your parents. If so, you're likely to have responded to them by showing compliance and withdrawal or with rage and rebellion. In either case, you were not given the chance to become adept at managing and resolving conflicts, accepting differences, and learning to express and regulate negative emotions.

If, instead, discipline was used as a means of guidance and teaching, you will have felt safe in your attachment to your parents and will have gained a respect for differences, the ability to discuss and resolve conflicts, and the knowledge of how to value not only your own wishes, beliefs, and behavior but also those of the other family members.

In healthy relationships between adults, discipline is not normally relevant. Discipline is for your children. However, the principles that you were taught as a child when your parents used discipline will have affected how you deal with differences, anger, and conflicts as an adult. Your experience of discipline is likely to have influenced whether you experience shame and rage or fear or despair in your relationship with your partner at times of conflict.

Theme 7: Being Close or Distant

Were your parents routinely available to assist you when you were struggling, to listen to you when you wanted to share an experience, or to just have fun together with you? Would you describe your parents as having been available, sensitive, and responsive? Were they unpredictable in their responsiveness for reasons often unknown to you or having nothing to do with you? Were they predictable in their lack of availability or emotional responsiveness to you? Would you describe your family as having been warm, cold, or somewhere in between?

During your childhood, your experiences within your family will have given you an idea of the role of relationships in your life. You were given a blueprint for the function of relationships and their importance. If your parents were often experienced as being extremely involved in their own personal lives and disinterested in their role as parents, you will have been left to manage your emotions and stressful events on your own and will have likely developed a dismissive attachment style. If your parents were present sometimes and others not—in a way that was unpredictable and confusing to you—you will likely have developed a preoccupied attachment style.

If you were raised in a family in which relationships primarily served a practical purpose and discussions functioned as a means for solving problems rather than an opportunity to share emotions and offer comfort and support, you might find that you tend to relate to your partner with a rather distant manner, dealing with problems and sharing thoughts but divulging little in the way of feelings. This can lead to conflict if your partner desires a greater focus on emotional communication and intimacy. Relationship detachment and ever increasing distancing will result if you and your partner are both inclined to avoid emotional intimacy.

In contrast, if your parents demonstrated emotional closeness with each other and with you while at the same time managing conflicts easily as they emerged, you are likely to seek such emotional closeness and to be reasonably good at attaining this in your relationships. You will seek a partner who desires and is competent in maintaining a close relationship with you.

Theme 8: Handling Loss

Did you experience any losses in the family during your childhood or adolescence? Were there any deaths? Was there a separation, or divorce? Were these events addressed openly? Did you receive support in dealing with them?

If you experienced losses in any of your attachment relationships as a child, these losses may well have undermined your sense of security, your belief that your other attachment relationships would be lasting. If your mother died or, following a divorce from your father, was not often present in your day-to-day life, you may have either begun to cling to your father, though perhaps with some ambivalence, or decided to protect yourself from another loss by avoiding emotional closeness with him.

Now in adulthood, you are likely to be at risk of having difficulty in your relationships, if losses that you experienced as a child were not openly addressed with your attachment figures who at the time provided you with support. If one or both of your parents thought it best to carry on as if the loss had never occurred, you will have had to struggle to go through and integrate the loss on your own. Its intensity and threat to your sense of self might well have proved to be too onerous for you to manage, causing you to enter a state of denial of your intense emotions.

If you endured major childhood losses and were not supported well at the time, you will be challenged in your ability to feel safe in important relationships in adulthood. You might become more controlling—giving yourself a false sense of security, a feeling that you can prevent the possibility of further losses—or more distant and detached so that you will be less hurt if the relationship ends.

However, if you experienced significant losses but were able to grieve those losses with the active emotional support of a parent or someone else with whom you had a strong attachment, there is a good chance that you were able to develop the emotional resiliency to manage loss. This will have fostered your ability to enter into healthy relationships as an adult in spite of your early losses.

Theme 9: Managing Traumatic Events

Were there any events that you would consider to have been traumatic (highly stressful)? Were these caused by your parents or other important adults? How did you manage such an event at the time? Did your parents or other important adults assist you in dealing with it?

While the loss of an attachment relationship in childhood is certainly traumatic, there are other events that can be just as traumatic. Among them are maltreatment, serious accidents or disease, major separations from the family, and significant betrayals, rejections, or assaults inflicted by individuals outside the family. If those to whom you were attached were the source of your trauma—if you suffered child abuse and neglect in the family—the trauma will have been particularly difficult to manage and resolve. If your attachment figures traumatize you, your sense of trust is greatly compromised—frequently leading to attachment disorganization—and you are subject to pervasive shame and terror. If your attachment figures do not provide you with safety, you somehow must provide it yourself.

The outcome of intrafamilial trauma is often the adoption of a dismissive or preoccupied attachment scheme. Further, while your general scheme of relating may reflect an autonomous attachment style, you may find yourself experiencing intense emotions or intrusive thoughts in situations that remind you of past trauma. Memories of the past may be activated by certain emotions, events, sensations, or activities in the present that make it difficult for you to remain engaged in your relationship in a healthy manner.

If particular situations cause your normally satisfying relationship to become stressful and a source of dysregulation, you might choose to stop and reflect on any pattern that you can identify in these troubling situations and see if you are able to make connections between the present and past. Such awareness may well be the first step toward helping you find ways to reduce the impact of past trauma on your current relationships.

Theme 10: Having Important Relationships with Other Adults

Were there adults in your life outside your immediate family who cared for you for significant periods of time? Were there adults you spent time with, learned from, and felt valued by and who helped you feel good about yourself and your life? Did these relationships enable you to change the meaning of your relationship with your parents in any way?

Turn your gaze from your family for a moment and focus on other important relationships in your childhood. If you are able to identify other important relationships you might reflect on what possible influence they may have had on your development. Those adults may well have helped you to have another perspective on your parents' thoughts, feelings, and behaviors as they related to you and your world. This is likely to have given you more options for making sense of your life as a child and to have helped you discover unique, positive qualities in yourself, different from—or not seen by—your parents.

The influence of nonparental adults on your development attests to the fact that while the influence of your parents is important in the development of your relationship styles, you are not

limited to those relationships alone. In fact, relationships throughout your life may influence subsequent relationships. If you have
healthy relationships with your friends, these relationships can be
of benefit to your relationship with your partner and vice versa.
Although you are influenced by your past, you are not determined
by it. If you are truly open to new relational experiences, they can
carry new meanings and relational abilities into the future.

Reexperiencing Your Past

We often are told to let sleeping dogs lie or that the past is past. My
response to the first is, Sleeping dogs may well awaken at the most
inopportune moments. Better to wake the dog when you're in a
position to care for it and tame it. And to the second I would say, If
the past were to stay in the past we would not have to take notice
of it. But the past constantly influences the meaning that we give
to the present. It would be better for the present to influence the
meaning that we give to the past.

Yes, the past is still alive in the present, and because of this, it
can be influenced, modified, deepened, and given new meanings. We cannot change the events of the past, but we can change
the meanings we give to them. By changing the meanings, we can
alter the influence of those past events on the present. In the process of effecting such changes, we often find that we can make
new sense of the past in ways that are liberating—ways that carry
hope for our current relationships, as well as those that lie in the
future.

Example

Sharon, age 29, struggles with self-criticism, with lack of career
satisfaction, and in relationships with partners; she loses interest
and withdraws, leaving the relationship after two or three months.
She remembers her childhood as being uneventful, though she
wishes she had been closer to her mother over the years. Her moth-

er was a busy professor, often at work on her research and with her students. Her parents divorced when Sharon was 7 years old, and while she did maintain contact with her father, this was infrequent, and she felt she was not important to him and subsequently concluded that he was not very important to her either.

Sharon developed a relationship with a woman her age, Melinda, in the next office at the large architecture firm where she worked. As they got to know each other, Sharon became increasingly open and relaxed, speaking of her interests and dreams, her history and her struggles. Sharon could not recall ever having had a friend like Melinda. She felt accepted by Melinda and found that she could say anything that she wanted and not feel judged by her. She found herself telling Melinda things that she had never told anyone. She spoke of problems that had emerged in her recent romantic relationships. She told Melinda that she was now doubting her own ability to become close to a man, whereas she previously had thought it was just that she had not found the "right" one. She also acknowledged that she was constantly looking over her shoulder at work, expecting to be criticized. She revealed all these things to Melinda, and still Melinda was her friend—doubts, inadequacies, and all.

In their conversations, Sharon was often puzzled by Melinda's responses. Melinda seemed to think that the relationship problems Sharon was describing were common and even necessary in the early stages of developing a more intimate relationship with someone. Melinda thought that when a potential partner of Sharon's expressed a difference with her it might be a sign of increased openness and sharing rather than proof that the person was critical of her and thought that she was wrong. Melinda also commented—almost in passing it seemed—that maybe Sharon's uncertainties around potential partners might have something to do with her lacking a meaningful relationship with her father. Sharon guessed that Melinda might be right about that but she had seldom thought about it. Sharon had thought of her relationship with her father as being a disappointment, but never really felt that it—or her father for that matter—had any influence on her current life. She believed that she had long recovered from his apparent indifference to her.

Melinda also mentioned that she had seen some of Sharon's work at the office and was impressed by it. On top of this, Melinda also said she sometimes heard others mentioning Sharon in a favorable light—they thought Sharon was an asset to the business. At first Sharon thought Melinda just wanted her to feel good and was making up what she said about her co-workers. Sharon had never imagined that Stan, who had worked with her on two important projects, thought that she had made major contributions to their work together. Had he expressed that and she had simply not heard him? She had felt that she might have been slowing down their work together and now Melinda said that Stan thought her contribution to the work was essential to its success!

Melinda also spoke with Sharon about some of Melinda's own doubts and worries. Melinda's parents had worked extremely hard when she was young, putting together a business that eventually became successful. Melinda had spent a lot of time with her grandmother, going to her grandmother's house after school and often having dinner with her when Melinda's parents worked late. Melinda had had many conflicts with her parents during adolescence and it was not until she was in college that she began to feel truly close to her parents, to experience their love and support for her, which had been subsumed by their focus on their business. One weekend her mother tearfully spoke with Melinda about the many times she had looked at Melinda's picture when she was working late, regretting that she was not home with Melinda to help her with her homework, prepare dinner for her, and teach her how to cook. Things seemed to begin to fall into place for Melinda after that. She never talked with her father the way she had begun to with her mother. But she had no doubts about her relationship with her dad. She knew—partly because of stories her mom told her about him—that his love for her was as strong as her mother's.

Sharon and Melinda not only talked about their worries and other concerns, but had many light moments together and discovered they had interests in common. Sharon found herself reflecting on Melinda's comments about Sharon's relationships and work. Her newfound perspectives, gained through Melinda, about these important areas of her life were unsettling. Memories from her past emerged involving her relationship with her mother. Sharon recalled that when she and her mother disagreed Sharon always felt that she herself was wrong and her mother was right. If they disagreed about something important—for example, Sharon's decision to go into architecture rather than history (her mother's preference)—she often felt that her mother was disappointed in her. She had assumed that unless she agreed with her mother, her mother would have less interest in her. She realized that she had begun to avoid conflict and was trying to please her mother, but that she never felt that she was successful at this. It was hard to have these thoughts about her mother and their relationship. She felt disloyal just by thinking this way. She had always admired her mother's successful career and there just didn't seem to be any room to criticize her. She had believed that her mother wanted what was best for Sharon—and still did—but Sharon now began to see that her mother's need to make sure things worked out for Sharon undermined Sharon's confidence in her own judgments and goals.

Gradually Sharon began to compare the perspectives on conflict, assertiveness, and her own worth that were held by her mother and by Melinda. It increasingly seemed to her that the lack of emotional closeness and sharing between her and her mother resulted much more from her mother's need to control her and to have Sharon meet her expectations than from Sharon's own selfishness and inadequacies. Her mother's disappointment in her related to her mother's narrow views about what was right for her and about Sharon's responsibilities as a daughter.

Sharon slowly realized that disagreements with a potential partner were not necessarily a sign of rejection or disappointment. She also realized that her feeling that her worth depended on getting the approval of her mother—something that seldom happened— had carried over into her career, where she was constantly seeking confirmation from others about her abilities, so much so that her performance suffered and she didn't focus much on whether she felt proud of what she had accomplished. She also realized that even when affirmations were given, she didn't take notice of them! As Sharon thought over her distant relationship with her father, she allowed herself to recall times during her childhood and adolescence when he had failed to call or keep his promise to visit. She slowly became aware that she had actually felt great pain over his apparent rejection of her and that she had simply stopped feeling the pain. She had been able to convince herself that it really didn't matter. She allowed herself to feel that pain again—though she was going on 30 she still felt the pain of the rejections that she had experienced 20 years ago. And she felt anger too. She had deserved better! She had not failed him as a daughter, he had failed her as a father.

As Sharon began to give new meanings to her past relationships with her parents and saw how those relationships affected her then and now, she also began to see the connections between the meanings she gave to her present relationships and to her career performance. She became aware of the possibilities of giving the events of the present alternative meanings. When a man she became acquainted with expressed a perspective on an event different from her own, she took a deep breath and asked what made him see it that way. After considering his response, she was able to further clarify her perspective. As time passed, sometimes this led to her seeing things his way and other times his seeing them her way—and sometimes they continued to differ, yet he still enjoyed being with her! Their relationship was able to contain different opinions! And as she focused less on her colleagues' views of her work and more on the work itself, she noticed that her results improved. She became more and more aware of her own skills. This awareness enabled her to be more open to the constructive criticism of her colleagues. While it was not always pleasant to hear—truly hearing praise was uncomfortable for her—it led to further improvement in her abilities and a more relaxed atmosphere at work.

While the changes outlined in this vignette about Sharon are certainly not as easy to accomplish as has been described, they are realistic. Change does happen when adults are open to an awareness of the events of their past and how they experienced them. As they increasingly comprehend that the experience of an event is not the event itself, they are increasingly able to change the meanings of past and present events which are now less rigidly connected.

Such openness to new meanings of our important past relationships is often facilitated by current important relationships. When Sharon felt accepted and enjoyed by Melinda, she became increasingly open to Melinda's experience of her and their relationship itself. She began to share her doubts and worries and to open herself to Melinda's experience of those aspects of herself. She came to sense a difference in her reactions when having conversations with Melinda from how she'd felt during similar conversations—or more frequently the lack of such conversations—with her mother. As a result she now had a new outlook on her parents, her past relationships with her parents, and how those relationships affected her now. She was more aware of her autobiography than she'd been previously. It became more integrated, and ways to rewrite the meaning of past and present events became apparent.

Making Sense of It All

Those who have studied the nature of attachment conclude that if you've been able to make sense of the events of your life—and the nature of your most influential relationships—and then develop a story that is organized and interwoven with different elements, you tend to be in the best position to develop healthy relationships. Through understanding the characteristics of our relationships with our parents and other caregivers and with teachers, mentors, and friends, we can understand the characteristics of our current relationships. We will be more aware of our strengths and the challenges of close relationships. We will have insight into what we like and do not like in relationships, how we interact with others, and how we want others to interact with us. From this awareness we are able to develop the best course of action for guiding the development and maintenance of our current relationships.

Let's suppose that you had a difficult relationship with your father. Imagine that he was often critical and seldom supportive in his manner of relating with you. He did not initiate much interaction and seemed preoccupied when you did something together. How might you have responded? Here are some possibilities:

- You avoided him and turned mostly to your mother for what you wanted and needed.
- You took great pains to please him and were often disappointed.
- You had frequent conflicts with him, forcing him to pay attention to you the only way that worked.
- You attempted to develop relationships with other men, at school or in the community.
- You generally devalued relying on others for your emotional needs and you devalued your emotional life itself.

How might you have made sense of his manner of relating with you? Here are some choices:

- You thought that your dad was a good father who had a lot of responsibilities and good reasons for not spending time with you and supporting your development.
- You thought you were lazy, bad, stupid, or limited in what you had to offer your father.
- You thought that men generally were like your father and you anticipated that other men would treat you the same way.
- You thought that your father was a poor parent who was not fair to you. You dwelled on his treatment of you and blamed him for most of the troubles in your life.
- You did not think about your father or your relationship with him

much. You tried to convince yourself that your relationship with him was not that important in your life.

Let's suppose that you made sense of the characteristics of your relationship with your dad and developed an organized story that looked something like this:

Now and then, you recall your relationship with your dad, remembering both the many difficult times and (if they occurred at all) the fewer enjoyable times. You made sense of his manner of relating with you by using one or more of these explanations:

- Relations with others, possibly with his children especially, were hard for him.
- He had a hard life as a child, particularly regarding his father, who had been critical and rejecting.
- His primary sources of pleasure were work, hobbies, and friends, not his children.
- He had difficulty dealing with conflict and expressing his emotions.
- He had wanted a closer relationship with you but he didn't know how to bring it about and he avoided thinking about it.

You made sense of the impact of your father's behavior on various aspects of your development in one or more of the following ways:

- You tend to be self-critical and to have considerable self doubt.
- You tend to be overly critical of others, noticing qualities that you dislike and failing to recognize qualities that you might like.
- You tend to become sad and discouraged easily.
- You tend to avoid conflicts or to have strong reactions to conflicts.
- You tend to overvalue or undervalue relationships as they develop.
- You tend to avoid emotional experiences, preferring a cognitive perspective.

Finally, let's consider some ways in which you might engage in relationships now if you have resolved any difficulties created in your relationship with your father and developed an autonomous attachment pattern:

- You are aware of the tendencies noted above, and you are able to reflect on them and reduce their influence over your current relationships.
- You have reflected on how other important people in your life have related to you, differentiated them from your relationship with your father, and used this awareness to give yourself confidence about what you have to offer in a relationship.
- You have developed an understanding of the value of conflict and how to manage it without damaging the relationship.
- You have reflected on how you want to be in a relationship and then deepened your strengths while reducing your challenges.
- You have learned to inhibit defensive tendencies that you developed in your relationship with your father and have remained open to new experiences in your relationships with your friends and partner.

While this example may give the impression that this process is easier than it actually is, it nevertheless is valuable as a guide for how we might best tailor our efforts toward building healthy relationships. Being able to face the difficult events of our past relationships, while managing the strong emotions associated with them, enables us to develop a realistic view of the strengths and weaknesses in how we relate to others as well as to understand what we are looking for in our meaningful relationships. The challenge is to openly reflect on those important past relationships so that the new meanings that we are able to develop may be our guide for developing healthy relationships now.

The challenges we face in making sense of our past often result from our difficulties in looking at those events with our parents or other people significant in our development. We may feel that it is selfish or disrespectful to be negative about how our parents raised us. Or when we begin to recall a past event involving our father, if we again feel any of the shame or fear that was originally associated with that event, we are unlikely to reflect on those experiences with a new perspective. So we restrict our memories and limit what they have to offer as a guide for our current relationships. Or we may have trouble recalling past events because they are associated with intense emotional states of fear, despair, or rage, causing us to avoid them or obsessively dwell on them. Or we obsess about past relationships, see them as preventing us from being able to have a good life now, and then do not notice new opportunities for relating with others. None of these approaches enables us to reflect on and learn from past events. If we fail to make sense of those events we are at risk of repeating them.

In summary, your autobiography is a living reality in your life. It can be rewritten in response to new thoughts and experiences, and especially new relationships. At the same time it influences how you experience relationships today. Understanding your autobiography is important because it helps you see how your past relationships influence your present ones and how your present relationships influence your perspective on your past ones. The result will offer the greatest potential for new relationships to meet your emotional and psychological needs.

Exercise

Now might be a good time to return to your responses to the questions under each of the 10 autobiographical themes that were presented earlier in the chapter.

Think of your relationship with one of your parents. Think of a current important relationship in your life. Think of similarities and differences between these characteristics as they existed with your parent (or other adult—number 10) and as they exist today with someone in your life.

1. How were positive emotions shared?
2. How were vulnerable emotions shared?
3. How was anger managed?
4. How were conflicts resolved?
5. How were differences treated?
6. What was the nature of discipline?
7. Were family members close or distant?
8. If you experienced losses were you supported?
9. Did you experience traumas and did you receive support in managing them?
10. Were there other adults who were important to you?

There certainly are likely to be similarities between your childhood attachment relationships and important relationships in your life now. If there are differences, what do you think led to them?

Think again about the events that characterized those early relationships with your parents. What meanings did you give to those events in the past? What other possible meanings could you give those events? If you accepted a new meaning to explain the past event, do you think that would change the way you relate to the person in your life today? In what way? Why do you think there would be a change?

Yes, our autobiography—especially with regard to our history of attachment relationships—is important in influencing the nature of our present and future relationships. The strength and pervasiveness of its importance is a result of the nature of our brains. The structure and functioning of our brains ensures that our relationships are extremely important in our lives. Our brains are designed for the development and maintenance of our relationships. When our brain is working at its best, our relationships tend to be at their best. So let us look inward again—this time into our brains—to better understand how to best develop our relationships.

KEY 3

KNOW YOUR BRAIN
AND BIOLOGY

By now you've probably caught on to the relevance of the first three words of the introduction: *Who are you?* This book continues to spend a good deal of time asking you to focus on yourself in order to better develop your skills for healthy relationships. Believe it or not, your biology, just as much as your autobiography, plays a crucial role in determining how you behave in your relationships. So what could be better to investigate than how your brain is designed for healthy relationships? Yes, if you allow your brain to develop the organizational structure and related functioning that it is capable of, you will find yourself surprisingly ready for healthy relationships.

The Brain's Social Engagement System

Let's begin with a brief description of the autonomic nervous system and how it manages our interactions with the world. This system begins in the brain stem and its nerve circuits extend into all parts of the body, especially to the heart, lungs, and gut. It works mostly without conscious awareness and its job is to manage things like breathing, heart rate, digestion, sweating, and sexual arousal, which would require too much time if they worked only when we told them to. This system determines whether you need to mobilize, that is, increase your heart rate and breathing and decrease your ability to digest food, or immobilize, decrease your heart rate and breathing, and increase the activity of your digestive system.

When you are not feeling safe and you sense that action is called for to keep yourself secure, your heart rate and breathing increase as you prepare for fighting or fleeing. If you are not feeling safe and you do not sense a course of action, you immobilize, your heart rate and breathing decrease, and you remain as motionless and vigilant as possible, with the hope that by hiding you might be safe or by remaining vigilant the best course of action will become apparent and you will spring into action. When you are not feeling safe, both systems—mobilized and immobilized— are functioning in a *defensive* manner. Their goal is to protect you in whatever way is possible. When in a defensive mode, the features of your brain necessary for being sensitive to another person and relating to him or her in the best possible way so as to develop a healthy relationship are not working! When it is defensive your brain is focused only on self-protection and you notice primarily expressions from the other person that might put you at risk— physically or psychologically.

Now, let us assume that you are feeling safe. Another circuit of the autonomic nervous system is activated—a system closer to the immobilization circuit (we might call it "quiet and aware"), mentioned above, than to the mobilization circuit—and a central function of this circuit is to enable you to successfully begin and maintain relationships with others. Not surprisingly, the neuropsychologist who has studied this system in the brain the most, Stephen Porges, refers to it as the *social engagement system*. When this neurological circuit is active—still connecting the brain with the heart, lungs, and gut—you are *open and engaged*, not defensive. When open and engaged, you are both sensitive to the subtle relationship cues of the other person and ready and able to relate to him or her in an attuned, responsive, and cooperative manner.

When open and engaged, your social engagement system gives priority to the human voice and facial expressions over other sources of auditory and visual sensations. You are able to detect subtle meanings in the modulations, pauses, rhythms, and varying levels of intensity in the voice of the person you are dealing with. You are able to detect similar meanings in subtle facial movements, especially around the eyes and mouth. To support these sources of knowledge, you are also very aware of the other person's gestures and movements. Thus, when you are open and engaged, the priority of your sensory motor skills and the associated nonverbal (or bodily) communications is to facilitate your ability to engage in healthy relationships. When you do not feel safe, you will be defensive and your primary sensory focus will be on picking up any signals that represent a threat to your safety. These constitute a narrow range of sensory input and you are prevented from picking up on a much wider range of sensory signals, which would facilitate entering into and maintaining a healthy relationship. When you're defensive, you give priority to signals from the other person that hint at threat and you're likely to fail to notice signals that suggest a positive attitude toward you and the relationship.

Notice that when you relax with a friend, sharing a meal together, for example, you find yourself using a conversational tone and a variety of vocal and facial expressions, which are rhythmic and synchronized with the expressions of your friend. If you were being observed by a scientist researching human relationships, this scientist might note that the movements of your head and that of your friend were echoing one another. The researcher would smile to see your friend reach up and scratch her head a split second after you did yours or notice you shift your posture just as your friend did. Such synchronization is not surprising because the social engagement system activates the nerves in the brain that connect to vocal and facial expressions and body movements. As you communicate with your friend in this open and engaged manner your expressions quickly synchronize for optimal understanding of each other. Your body tells you about the mind of your friend before your mind becomes aware of it. Being safe, you also notice that your friend's bodily expressions indicate that she is feeling safe too! Seeing that, you feel even more safe with her, and she with you, and so on.

Let's move further into the implications of how your brain is designed for relationships. As noted above, the best way to activate this open and engaged state of mind, the most effective state of mind for healthy relationships, is to feel safe with the other person. And to optimize this sense of safety? *Acceptance!* Yes, when you feel that you are being accepted, not evaluated, by your friend, you are much more likely to remain open and engaged, rather than defensive. Acceptance enables you to feel that your friend is comfortable with you. You do not have to be careful with your friend. You are able to spontaneously express your thoughts, feelings, and wishes and you will not be judged. And the same holds true for your friend. When you communicate acceptance of her, she will feel safe and be open and engaged with you.

At the core of all healthy relationships is acceptance, not evaluation. Your interactions are simply focused on sharing your ideas or interests, not on judging whether the other's thoughts or behaviors could be "improved." As soon as evaluation enters the arena, you or your friend will drift into a defensive state of mind, which restricts the ability to truly enjoy and be present with each other. You won't be surprised to hear that the best way to communicate acceptance of the other person is to express yourself using a full range of modulations and rhythm in your voice and expressiveness in your face. As you restrict this range of expression and your voice becomes a monotone or your face has a flat expression, the other person begins to feel evaluated by you. No wonder lectures and unasked-for advice tend to have little effect. Or if they do have an effect, it's to make people defensive.

Certainly there is a place and need for evaluations in healthy relationships. When something in your friend's behavior proves difficult for you to accept, your comment on his behavior would be considered to be an evaluation. Knowing that the evaluation will put a strain on the relationship, you're likely to inhibit its expression unless you believe the behavior itself is a bigger threat to the relationship. Such evaluations are necessary and too often avoided because of this threat, although the long-term threat of saying nothing is likely to be greater.

When evaluations are embedded in acceptance, when most of the interactions communicate acceptance rather than evaluation, then periodic evaluations may generate some strain on the relationship but, in the long run, be beneficial. Also, it is best that the evaluations are focused on the other's behavior, rather than what you think about any thoughts, feelings, or motives that might lie behind the behavior. If the other believes that you have a negative view of his inner life—his motives, for example—he is likely to be much more defensive than if he knows that it is only certain behaviors that you are evaluating.

For example, if your friend makes a promise to you and fails to keep it, you might say (without judgment), "I'm disappointed because you said that you would change the appointment time and you didn't do it. Why didn't you?" Your friend is likely to apologize and give a reason and try to repair any harm done to the relationship. Imagine, however, if your evaluation included your guess about your friend's motive: "I'm disappointed because you said that you would change the appointment time and you didn't do it. You really don't value our friendship very highly." If you made that comment (with its assumption about your friend's not valuing the friendship), your friend is less likely to be motivated to apologize or work to repair the relationship.

You might think I'm referring to only negative evaluations, but in this discussion I include positive evaluations, or praise. When you praise another person he is likely to become mildly defensive. If you're judging him positively at this moment, you could just as easily judge him negatively the next. Or he may take your praise to imply that you expect him to function at the same level of whatever the positive trait is all the time. He may sense that you would not accept him if he slipped or was in a bad mood. If he believes that you only spend time with him because he's always good, he's not likely to feel accepted for who he is.

Of course there is value in praising your friend. But best to keep the praise a small part of your expressions, with most of the expressions conveying acceptance. Also best if you express praise spontaneously, with animation, rather than as a monologue judgment that communicates that something he did was of worth. Your praise then simply reflects your expressive enjoyment and shared pride in some of his features that represent aspects of who he is and what is important to him. You also are best expressing praise with no strings attached. If the intention of your praise is to induce your friend to show the behavior again, your friend is likely to not respond to it or to respond defensively.

You see, the social engagement system in your brain is designed for safe, meaningful, and enjoyable relationships. When you are open and engaged when interacting with your friend, the friendship is likely to deepen. You are communicating that your friend is important to you, you are interested in him and what he shares with you, and you are fully present with him in your interactions.

From *Me* to *We*

There have been significant advances in our understanding of the human brain over the past 25 years as a result of extensive research utilizing new technology. Daniel Siegel and Allan Schore, both at the University of California, Los Angeles, have studied the directions in which this knowledge has led us. They have proposed a new field of study, known as interpersonal neurobiology. The comprehensive findings about how the brain works demonstrate what was said earlier: The brain was designed for relationships. Not only do healthy relationships serve as a source of great pleasure in our lives, they also are crucial to the development of our brains—and our minds. Here, following Siegel, we will consider *mind* to represent the flow of energy and information that occurs in the brain. Siegel's book, *The Developing Mind*, presents the findings of numerous studies that demonstrate that healthy relationships are crucial for the organization of the brain, helping it function at its best and integrating awareness taken from the body, the mind, and relationships.[1] Relationships are the source of extensive knowledge that is not available to us without the perspectives and experiences that are shared with us in a reciprocal, open, and engaged relationship.

Siegel speaks of the crucial move from *me* to *we* in the development of the person, the family, the culture, and society. We are a social species. When we function in a manner that best develops these social skills we not only survive but also thrive. Within the state of *we*, your inner life—your thoughts, emotions, intentions, values, perceptions, memories, and beliefs—becomes integrated with the inner life of your partner or friend, and your resulting understanding of your shared attention takes on greater depth and breadth. These relationships are reciprocal. You influence each other. You each bring something to the event you are sharing and you take much more away from it. Your understanding together is much greater than the sum of what you would understand separately if you did not share. Yes, you have neurological systems in your brain specifically designed for healthy relationships.

Siegel proposes the concept of "resonance circuitry" in the brain that enables you to be attuned to, in sync with, your friend, an experience in which your body and mind are deeply aware of the experience of the other, just as his body and mind are aware of your experience. This circuitry involves the prefrontal cortex and anterior cingulate cortex, regions of your brain which function as a bridge between your thinking and your emotions, his thinking and his emotions and you and him, integrating all in a manner that creates empathy and compassion for your friend. This circuitry is enhanced by related neurological entities known as mirror neurons, which enable your mind to resonate with the mind of the other person when you perceive the intentional actions of the other and tend to respond in kind (your friend scratches his head and you find yourself doing the same; your friend has an expression of sadness and you experience a similar sadness). The anterior cingulate cortex, especially around a specialized re-

1. D. J. Siegel, *The developing mind: How relationships and the brain interact to shape who we are* (2nd ed.) (New York: Guilford Press, 2011).

gion known as the insula, creates your capacity for gaining intuition into your friend's experience and a related ability to feel empathy. Further connections to the amygdala, hippocampus, and thalamus bring a rich emotional component to our relationships. All of these areas are activated and maintained by neurotransmitters such as oxytocin (producing the desire to be near) and dopamine (causing pleasure from being near).

Enough about these neurological circuits and regions. What is their significance? They ensure that we both need and enjoy healthy relationships, and must have them if we want to have the best chance at a meaningful, enjoyable, and integrated life. Research tells us that healthy relationships feature reciprocity—sharing and taking turns. Healthy relationships are meaningful to both members of the relationship, who both contribute to its value. These relationships involve compassion and empathy. The separate experiences of each member are accepted and valued. They are not based on obedience and compliance. The social-emotional experience of one person is not "right" while that of the other is "wrong."

Intersubjectivity: From Infants to the Elderly

The effects of this resonating circuit in the brain are evident in the interactions between a parent and infant. They are in sync. Their nonverbal articulations—vocalizations, facial expressions, gestures, and movements—have the characteristics of dance. This constellation of interactions has been called the "dance of attunement," with *attunement* referring to the nonverbal expressions of emotional states that become synchronized with each other.

Healthy relationships at all ages possess the same characteristics. When nonverbal expressions are developed and expressed in unison for a long time, partners begin to look like each other, move in synchrony without any intention of doing so, and read each other's minds before a word is said. In such relationships there is little to differentiate what is best for one from what is best for the other. There is reason to believe that both the structure and the functioning of the brains of those two partners are increasingly similar as the years go on.

There is a more encompassing term for this dance of attunement, one that describes additional qualities of this connection between a parent and baby—and people of any age who are closely related. The term is *intersubjectivity*. Intersubjectivity refers to attunement but also to two other traits. In the first, two individuals are aware of and pay attention to an event that holds meaning for them both. This event might be a joint memory, the story one is telling the other, their relationship, the condition of an ill friend, a movie they are watching together, a song, a flower, or a passing stranger's interesting hat. The focus of their attention is having an effect on both of them, whether the effect is deeply meaningful to both, as in the health of the joint friend, or of light and transient meaning, as in the stranger's hat. Whatever it is, it is holding the attention of both and affecting both.

Besides attunement and joint attention, intersubjectivity refers to having a common purpose, a shared reason for being together and doing something together. This common purpose might be exemplified in cooperating in or bringing each other's interests, skills, and energy to an activity. Such common purpose often results in more meaning, enjoyment, and success in whatever is being pursued together. When this common purpose is simply to be together, to share something together, to enjoy being together, or to learn something together, it is clear that the relationship is of value to both parties. Both are contributing to the relationship and the enjoyment of one is crucial for the enjoyment of the other. When there is no sense of attunement, when the two friends are focusing on different things, or when they have different motives for being together, intersubjectivity is not present. In this case, the relationship itself is not likely to develop further. In fact, the relationship might be damaged if one person's interests and motives are valued and the other's are not, or if one is dominant and the other is submissive, or if a lack of intersubjectivity continues for too long.

Intersubjective experiences are inherently of value to healthy relationships, since they, by the very definition of intersubjectivity, create a secure sense of knowing that the experiences of both individuals are important, are noticed, and have an impact on the other and the relationship. Both are contributing and both benefit from being together. The sense of attunement one with the other creates an experience of emotional intimacy that carries deep pleasure and meaning.

Intersubjective experiences foster the development of the social-emotional areas in the brain, the prefrontal and anterior cingulate cortices of both members of the relationship. Safety is ensured because there is a deep awareness that the mind is dealing with experience, and neither partner is right or wrong. All experiences are valued as each experience brings another perspective to an event to foster a more clear and comprehensive understanding of it for both you and your partner.

It is often this intersubjective experience that one member of a relationship is seeking when that person approaches the partner or friend to share something exciting and enjoyable or sad and worrisome. Feeling attuned with this friend, the person is not alone in the emotional experience. In such intersubjective states, excitement and joy are often amplified, whereas worries and sadness are lightened. In focusing on the event together, understanding of the event increased, in turn leading to more comprehensive insights and perspectives. Having a common purpose frequently creates a greater sense of hope and confidence or a sense of completeness about what has occurred.

Your Integrated Brain

When we combine our understanding of being open and engaged rather than defensive with what we know about resonating circuits, we come to an important realization regarding the moment-to-moment interactions in our relationships. If you approach your friend in an open and engaged manner and your friend approaches you in a defensive manner, because of the nature of our tendency to resonate with the emotional state of the other person, within minutes you will either both be open and engaged or both be defensive. Your state tugs on the state of your friend and vice versa.

Either you will change to meet and match the state of your friend or your friend will do so toward you.

The danger is that it is more likely that both of you will become defensive rather than open and engaged. If you're defensive—by definition, not feeling safe—your lack of safety will provoke a similar sense of threat in your friend. The need for safety takes precedence over a desire to be open and engaged with your friend or any other aspect of your existence.

So what to do? This is a bit tricky, but if you're able to remain aware of what's happening—notice that your friend is defensive—you will be able to inhibit your tendency to become defensive yourself and remain open and engaged. By reflecting on your friend, his defensiveness, and the current situation, you may become aware that you are in fact still safe and do not need to become defensive yourself. Through inhibiting your defensive tendency and remaining open and engaged, your friend is likely to gradually realize that he is safe and need not be defensive. This may activate a similar tendency within him to be open and engaged with you. It is that first moment—inhibiting your tendency to react to his defensiveness in kind—that is the crucial moment. Your ability to reflect on what is happening (something that we will explore in greater depth in the next chapter) that makes the difference.

So, you may ask, how do you develop the ability to inhibit your tendency to become defensive when your friend is? Simply develop the strength and organization of your dorsolateral prefrontal cortex. And how do you do that? Through having healthy relationships throughout your life and through developing your abilities to remain mindfully aware of your experiences when with others. Rest assured in the knowledge that is never too late to start. Your brain is likely to respond and strengthen when you use it in ways that it was meant to be used, for years to come.

Example
Robert and Diane have been dating for a few months. They meet for lunch, and while they are waiting for their order, Robert asks

Diane if she'd like to go to a movie on Friday night. Diane replies that she wishes she could but she already has a commitment that night.

ROBERT: *(With mild irritation.)* That's the second time you turned me down. If you'd rather not see me anymore I'd appreciate it if you just told me. I'm old enough to know.

DIANE: *(Quickly matching his irritation.)* I just said that I'm busy Friday night. Just because we've been seeing each other for a while doesn't mean that you can expect me to set aside all my free time for you.

ROBERT: Now you're saying I'm too controlling. I guess that I'm right, that you're finding reasons for not getting together. You don't have to make up stuff, just tell me.

DIANE: I'm not making up anything. I never thought you were until this conversation, but now I think you *are* too controlling.

Robert's defensiveness and confrontation elicited Diane's defensive response. If Robert had approached Diane with his doubts in an open and engaged manner, most likely she would have replied in kind.

ROBERT: That's the second time you've said no, and I worry that you might be thinking of ending our relationship.

DIANE: Not at all, Robert. I'm enjoying our time together a great deal. I actually wish that I didn't have the other commitments so I could go to the movie with you.

ROBERT: I'm a bit insecure. You already mean a lot to me. I hope that you're able to accept my doubts.

DIANE: No problem. You just don't know me well enough to see all *my* insecurities.

Or if Diane was able to inhibit her defensive response to Robert's defensiveness, he may have been able to become open and engaged himself.

ROBERT: *(With mild irritation.)* That's the second time you turned me down. If you'd rather not see me anymore I'd appreciate it if you just told me. I'm old enough to know.

DIANE: If I've given you any impression, Robert, that I want to end our relationship, I'm sorry. I don't feel that way at all.

ROBERT: Thanks. I just get insecure at times. You mean a lot to me already.

DIANE: It's nice hearing you say that—that I mean a lot, not that you're insecure. Of course insecure is also fine, since I am too.

Two Brains Together

The next time your partner or friend asks you what you want out of your relationship, you might reply: "Actually I am hoping that our anterior cingulate and prefrontal cortex develop in synchrony with similar organizational structures and functions, that our amygdalas generate a desire to approach each other and create pleasure for us both when we are together, and that our insula and mirror neurons thrive when we are together. Finally, I truly am looking forward to the pleasure that comes from our nucleus accumbens activating together and transmitting a lovely flow of dopamine in our brains when we share our experiences and our lives together."

A bit much—unless you're a neurobiology geek—but accurate nonetheless. I have actually written a book about this with a good friend of mine, Jon Baylin, who might be described as somewhat of a neurobiology fan. The title is *Brain-Based Parenting*, and while it focuses on the systems of the brain that are central in effective parenting, the conclusions are valid for all important relationships.[2]

There are five systems in a parent's brain that, when activated, enable him or her to engage in good parenting for months or years. These systems are very similar to five systems in the child's

2. D. Hughes and J. Baylin, *Brain-based parenting: The neuroscience of caregiving for healthy attachment* (New York: W. W. Norton, 2012).

brain that enable the child to develop a secure attachment with his or her parents. These systems involve the regions of the brain just mentioned above. They are the following:

- The *approach* system, which involves the desire to be with your parent/child and is activated by oxytocin and a few related neurotransmitters.
- The *reward* system, which brings pleasure to the interaction and involves the release of dopamine when engaged with your parent/child.
- The *child-reading* (or *parent-reading*) system, which evokes deep interest in your parent/child and sensitizes you to attend to his or her expressions and thus understand him or her better.
- The *meaning-making* system, which leads you to see the meaning and value of your relationships with your child/parent and to see these in your specific interactions.
- The *executive* system, which enables you to make sense of it all and maintain the relationship through thick and thin with one eye on your long-term goals (to raise your child well and to maintain a long-term relationship).

A fascinating and important reality about these five systems is that they are designed to work best when they work in synchrony with the other person. The activation of these systems and regions of the brain are reciprocal. When your child does not respond to you, it becomes harder to continue to initiate all those systems—approaching your child, experiencing pleasure in the interactions, being interested in your child, seeing positive meaning in the interactions and the relationship, and being able to carry on in the relationship over a long period of time. The same is true for the child if the parent does not respond to his or her attachment-based initiatives. And—this is the primary reason for mentioning these systems in this book—the same is true for good friends or partners in healthy relationships. Your brain works best and you relate best when the energy, delight, and fascination that you bring to your important relationships are matched in kind by your friend or partner.

Male and Female Brains

While the brains of women and men are for the most part similar, it is important to consider some differences—and their implications—that also exist. While the origins of these differences might be varied, they nevertheless may be influential in the development of healthy relationships.[3]

> On average, women tend to have greater understanding of, and empathy for, the experiences of others. This relates to higher levels of both estrogen and oxytocin in women than in men. Oxytocin tends to increase our sensitivity to the facial expressions around another person's eyes, which enables us to read the other's emotions more accurately.

> On average, a man's brain works in a more "lateralized" manner, meaning that the man tends to use either the right or the left side of the brain at one moment in time, while the woman is more likely to use both sides at the same time. This tends to make the male brain more efficient—specialized—while the woman's brain is more integrative and more capable of "multitasking." This may relate to the fact that the back part of a woman's corpus callosum is likely to be larger than a man's, leading to greater cross-hemisphere "communication."

> A woman's anterior cingulate tends to be larger than a man's, again supporting women's tendency to be more attentive to and attuned with the other's emotional state.

> A woman's hippocampus, which is rich in estrogen receptors, tends to be larger than a man's. This leads to greater strength in social memory and contextualized memories of relationships.

> A man's amygdala tends to be larger than a woman's. The amygdala is rich in testosterone receptors that increase the readiness to react to situations with assertiveness, aggression, and competition.

While it is important to be aware of these tendencies and their contribution to strengths and weaknesses in our relationships, we

---

3. My friend and colleague Jon Baylin contributed most of this information.

should keep in mind that they are only tendencies and not excuses for relationship failings.

Promote the Social Engagement System with PACE

Now that we've thought about the brain and the social engagement system, the next step is to apply this awareness to our efforts to establish healthy relationships. How do we keep ourselves open and engaged rather than defensive? The answer, I believe, lies in being able to maintain an attitude of quiet awareness of the other person, while inhibiting any defensive reactions. We might consider how we relate with infants in order to better describe this attitude.

Infants are primarily sensory and emotional beings. We remain engaged with them and communicate with them primarily by synchronizing our bodily expressions and emotions with theirs. Knowing what we know about the importance of safety in infant development, we can assume that our engagement with them will be more effective if we are able to help them feel safe and thus open and engaged.

Reflecting on how I was with my children when they were infants, I became aware of four major features of my engagement with them: playfulness, acceptance, curiosity, and empathy, or PACE. It might help us to explore the role these features play in developing and maintaining our important relationships at *all* ages.

Before looking at these PACE features we might mention briefly how they activate and integrate regions of the brain that are crucial for the ongoing functioning of the social engagement system. *Playfulness* primes us to experience delight and the positive experiences of surprise in relationships; it generates dopamine and fosters ongoing pleasure in relationships. Playfulness then combines with *acceptance*, which neuropsychologist Stephen Porges has identified as the primary relational attitude for triggering the social engagement system, and the two prime the amygdala to anticipate a positive experience when we interact with our friend or partner. *Curiosity*, which calms the amygdala, encourages the hippocampus to allow us to understand our present situation; the temporal lobes then play a role, as mirror neurons, mentioned earlier, allow us to experience what our friend is expressing. Curiosity also activates the dorsolateral prefrontal cortex, which helps us reflect on our inner life and the inner life of our partner. Finally, *empathy* involves the activation of all aspects of our prefrontal cortex, along with our insula (where we sense the inner life of the other) within the anterior cingulate cortex. When empathy is active in combination with curiosity, both the affective and reflective components of our brain are involved, and we are much better able to remain open and engaged as we relate with our partner.

Playfulness

Imagine being with your baby and not becoming playful. (This, of course, does not apply to when your baby is in distress—that's where empathy comes in.) When you're engaged with your baby, you tend to be more animated than usual, using more expressive gestures and facial expressions, your voice rising in pitch and expressing modulations and rhythms typically not present in daily discourse. If your infant does not respond or did at first but is now looking away, your playfulness decreases, but it remains available for when the baby signals that he or she would like that playful engagement again.

At all ages, playfulness conveys a sense of hope and optimism that carries your relationship into the future. It conveys your overriding sense of enjoyment of the other person, regardless of any differences that might emerge. It communicates a sense of relaxed safety and closeness that is not as intense as direct signs of affection but that also conveys the positive meaning of the relationship to you. While playfulness may not be evident during times of distress, its return when the difficult time has passed demonstrates that the relationship remains, causing as much pleasure and enjoyment as ever. Without this background of playfulness for when things are going well, the hard times of stress in a relationship are likely to become harder, sometimes placing the relationship itself at risk.

Playfulness doesn't involve telling jokes during hard times for the purpose of distracting the other person from his or her distress. Playfulness occurs naturally during the ebb and flow of your engagement, often creating a casual sense of safety and enjoyment, the background for ongoing interactions.

Example

Judy has just spoken to Anne about a recent conflict with a man she is dating, a conflict similar to others she's had with him in the past. Anne has experienced empathy for her friend and expressed it, squeezing Judy's hand. Without thinking, Judy says:

JUDY: So help me understand, Anne, truthfully, why do we keep working on these relationships with guys who really do seem to be from another planet?

ANNE: Do you want the short version or the long one?

JUDY: Give me the short one.

ANNE: To promote interplanetary dialogue.

JUDY: And the long version?

ANNE: To activate our prefrontal cortex and anterior cingulate cortex and thus develop our brains to the fullest as we were told in that dull book on relationships that was written by a man.

JUDY: Maybe better to learn a new recipe for preparing shrimp.

Acceptance

It is usually so easy to accept every quality of your baby. An accepting attitude enables you to be open and engaged with whatever your baby does, responding in a synchronized manner without any effort to change him or her. Your infant, in turn, feels consistently safe in your presence, giving easy expression to impulses and intentional movements. As your child develops, you are sure to start evaluating his or her behaviors as part of your efforts to facilitate the youngster's socialization. However, it is wise to continue to fully accept your child's inner life and restrict your evaluations to his or her behavior alone; this is beneficial to both your relationship with your child and to his or her psychological development.

Much of the safety inherent in healthy relationships emerges from the for-better-or-worse quality of your relationship, which is facilitated through acceptance. Evaluations and conflicts regarding behavior are much more likely to be managed and resolved if you know that your friend is focusing on your behavior, not your inner life. When you sense that your friend is disappointed only in your behavior, not in who you are, you are much more likely to openly talk about a problem with your friend.

Similarly, when you and your friend are able to accept each other's thoughts and emotions, you are much more likely to be able to share and deepen each other's reflective and emotional experiences. Shared thoughts and emotions, when they are accepted and regulated, tend to deepen relationships through moving your interactions below the surface into what are the most personal and meaningful features of the relationship.

The value of acceptance applies not only to your ability to communicate emotions to each other but also to your readiness to become aware of emotions within yourself. If you are angry with your friend but are not willing to acknowledge your anger to yourself, you will be less able to use your anger as a guide for understanding your current experience of the friendship as well as what might be the best way to continue the relationship into the future. Acceptance of your inner life enables you to be more aware of it and to use this awareness to guide your future choices and behaviors.

Example
Abbie is having dinner with her partner, Brent, after a hard day at the office.

ABBIE: Sometimes I just feel worn out by the repetitive nature of what I do. Like, where's the meaning of it all? Where's the enjoyment? It makes me want to move to Tahiti and enjoy life with only having to worry about when to get up in the morning and where to fish and gather coconuts.

BRENT: What a lovely idea! I can see why it would be so appealing after your day today.

ABBIE: And maybe even—when I really feel like achieving the max—I'll look for a pineapple for dessert.

BRENT: And I'll build a sand castle, big enough to sit in while we feast.

ABBIE: What a great image. Let's work on that after we pay off the car, and the house, and get our kids into Harvard.

BRENT: Deal.

They laugh and their dreams turn toward their future kids and the adventures that await with them. Abbie feels a lot better, and her job seems more meaningful and less stressful. Her inner life and its expression, accepted by her and Brent, served its purpose.

Imagine a different dialogue, one in which Abbie's thoughts, feelings, and dreams were not accepted by Brent:

ABBIE: Sometimes I just feel worn out by the repetitive nature of what I do. Like, where's the meaning of it all? Where's the enjoyment? It makes me want to move to Tahiti and enjoy life with only having to worry about when to get up in the morning and where to fish and gather coconuts.

BRENT: You'd probably get bored with that within a week.

ABBIE: I'd like to try.

BRENT: That's fine. But I think that you'd better first manage the responsibilities that you've taken on if we're going to achieve our goals.

ABBIE: Maybe we should just change our goals.

BRENT: It's not going to happen. Adolescence ended 10 years ago.

ABBIE: Thanks for that. That really makes me feel lucky to be so "mature" and "responsible."

In this example, Brent did not accept Abbie's expressed thoughts, feelings, and fantasies, responding as if she had told him that her behavior was about to change radically (as though she had said she'd taken steps to move to Tahiti without first hearing his ideas and getting his agreement). Reminding her of her real-life obligations, Brent was critical of her inner life. Abbie was left feeling alone with the frustrations of her current life, and her commitments were likely to remain as obligations, with no infusion of meaning and positive dreams about her life with her children to come.

When we experience acceptance of any negative thoughts, feelings, or wishes we might have about our lives, we are more likely to be able to come around to the positive qualities of our lives. Challenging those negative thoughts and feelings tends to leave the actual negative features of our lives in the forefront of our minds with no space for any positive features.

Curiosity

Once you begin to accept your inner life and the inner life of your friend, you are in a position to be curious about them, without judgment. If you judge your thoughts and feelings to be "wrong," "selfish," or "bad," you are much less likely to be aware of them. Or if you notice them, your negative judgments about them lead you to only think about ways to eliminate them, rather than leading you to understand them. A general attitude of nonjudgmental wondering about your emotions will enable you to make sense of them, of their origins and their place in your autobiography, as well as what they say about you and your friend or partner in your current relationship. Maintaining the same curious stance in the immediate here-and-now situation will enable you to reflect on what is happening in order to make sense of it, rather than reacting to it. Why become angry with something your friend says or does (unless, of course, it is clearly assaultive) before knowing what it means?

Example

David was a veterinarian who found his profession increasingly less satisfying over the three years that had passed since he opened his practice. He spoke about his frustrations to his partner, Richard:

DAVID: I just don't enjoy going to the office at all anymore. It makes me so discouraged to think that I'll be doing this for the next 35 years.

RICHARD: What do you think are the hardest things about your work?

DAVID: What does it matter? I have to do it. I have all my loans to pay off and I'm not likely to make a better income without going back to school and starting over, and that's not going to happen.

RICHARD: But if you had a better sense of what you don't like about what you're doing . . .

DAVID: I find that if I dwell on something I don't like, that just makes it worse. Let's talk about something else.

In this example, David was not curious about his difficult working experience out of the belief that since he did not think that he had any choice but to continue to work, it was a waste of time to try to make sense of why it was so unsatisfying to him. His decision to keep working caused him to believe that wondering about his negative experiences with working would not be helpful. Imagine if he had taken another approach, valuing instead the importance of wondering about his inner life experience.

DAVID: I just don't enjoy going to the office at all anymore. It makes me so discouraged to think that I'll be doing this for the next 35 years.

RICHARD: What do you think are the hardest things about your work?

DAVID: I don't know, really. I still seem to get satisfaction when I can figure out what's wrong with the animal and plan the best treatment. I don't know if I enjoy the owner's relief and happiness more or my own satisfaction from helping the animal get well.

RICHARD: Is it hard when you're not able to help and the animal gets worse or dies?

DAVID: Yes, that's hard, but that's not the problem. I know I can't do miracles, and helping the owner with the prognosis and reducing the animal's pain is still satisfying. I think the problem is more . . . when the owner seems not to care. That's it. Even worse, when the owner's behavior is causing harm to the animal in the first place and the owner doesn't change his or her behavior. That's it! Some are so clueless. They don't seem to want to learn. I'm more invested in their pet than they are.

RICHARD: Anything that you can do about that?

DAVID: Not with some of them. But maybe with others. Maybe I could do a pet care course! Maybe even insist that if owners want me to treat their animal, they have to sign up for periodic instruction in better care for their pet. Of course I might lose some customers. But maybe I can find a way to get more of the owners more knowledgeable and involved in their pets' care. Let me think about that!

RICHARD: Sounds like the next 35 years don't seem as hopeless.

DAVID: Maybe not! Actually, now that I feel free to wonder about alternatives and have a better sense of what's bothering me . . . I seem to enjoy working with farm animals most. Maybe because the few farmers I work with are really committed to the health of their animals. Let me think about that too. Maybe there would be value in working more with them. Even developing a specialty that would be of value to farmers! I have a lot of thinking I want to do.

The not-knowing, completely open stance that I am suggesting for curiosity tends to deepen your self-awareness in ways that guide you in discovering other approaches to problems or conflicts. Being curious, with no limits on where your questions or thoughts might take you, might well lead to possibilities in your relationships or your life that are much more satisfying than your present course of action.

Empathy

Empathy follows immediately on your increasing understanding of the meaning of your interaction—how it connects to your inner life and the inner life of your friend—and your readiness to simply accept, rather than evaluate, it. Empathy enables you to be with your friend in his or her distress, providing support that enables your friend to manage it better and then leads to its resolution. As the distressful emotions remain regulated, you are likely to be able to reflect better on the situation and learn ways to better deal with it in the future. Empathy may also be directed toward yourself and your own distressful emotions so that you are able to experience compassion for yourself and the challenges you are struggling with.

Empathy represents the joining of your experience of your friend with your friend's experience of him- or herself. It serves to deepen your understanding of your friend in ways that reason cannot approach. It also serves to deepen your sense of his or her emotional state in a way that conveys to your friend that you truly get it. Since empathy conveys both reflective and emotional elements, it tends to be best communicated with clear and coherent nonverbal and verbal communications.

Empathy joins well with curiosity in assisting your friend to make sense of an event through reflecting on it with you, experiencing your compassion and your deep interest in understanding your friend's experience. You might find that with some friends, your periodic expression of empathy is sufficient for them to carry the discussion further, leading to greater insight and resolution. With other friends, you might notice that by combining your empathy with curiosity you are better able to assist them in telling their story.

Example

Karen is quite upset when she gets off the phone after a conversation with her sister. She tells her partner, Tim, that her sister has decided that she is not able to go with Karen on a trip to Europe next summer, a trip they had been planning for the past six months. Scenario One (Tim provides his judgment about the situation and gives advice):

KAREN: She gave me three reasons why she wasn't going, and I guess I understand.

TIM: How outrageous! Whatever her reasons, she should have tried harder to make it happen! She knew how important that was to you. She's just thinking of herself.

KAREN: You're being hard on her, Tim. She really feels badly about having to cancel. She must have said that she's sorry a hundred times.

TIM: Easy to say you're sorry and not try to make it happen.

KAREN: She did try, Tim. She tried a lot.

TIM: Why don't the three of us sit down and look at the options. I'll be able to come up with something that works.

KAREN: No, Tim. Thanks, but that won't help.

TIM: Well, it just seems that she's been forgetting about you a lot over the past few years. Maybe she has to learn that she can't just take you for granted.

KAREN: You're making her sound awful, Tim. She's my sister and I know her pretty well. These things just happen and we'll get through it. We love each other.

TIM: Just so it's not all of your giving and her taking.

KAREN: Let's change the topic. This isn't helpful.

Scenario Two (Tim expresses empathy for Karen. As he sits with her in her distress, she is able to come to some sense of what she wants to do):

KAREN: She gave me three reasons why she wasn't going, and I guess I understand.

TIM: How hard this must be for you! I know how much you've been looking forward to it.

KAREN: I think I've gone on the Internet a hundred times looking up ideas for what we could do and where we could go.

TIM: How disappointed you must be!

KAREN: I saw this as a great chance for us to get close to each other again. Like we were when we were in college.

TIM: So it was more than the trip itself. It was also your relationship with Jill. She's so important to you and it looks like you were hoping to share a lot of wonderful experiences with her again.

KAREN: Yes! I really did! She used to be my best friend as well as my sister and I hoped that we'd feel that way toward each other again.

TIM: She's so special to you.

KAREN: Yes, she is. She really is. We have to find a way to have what we had in the past. We have to find a way to feel that way again. Europe or not.

TIM: I can hear in your voice how much you want that. And I can hear that you'll find a way to make it happen.

Tim, in responding with only empathy, helped Karen in her efforts to express and manage her distress, understand how much and why she was so bothered by the change in her plans, and begin to think of how she might go forward. If Tim had responded to her distress with a lot of questions and then given advice, Karen may well not have been able to begin the process of managing her distress and reflecting on the future as well as she did. Experiencing and communicating empathy is often the primary means of being helpful when our partner is in distress.

Exercises

In any relationship, keeping the social engagement system rather than the defensive system activated will enable us to deal with disagreements or challenges in the best possible manner (assuming that we are not in physical danger, in which case defensiveness is preferable).

Think of a time when you approached your partner or friend in a defensive manner when you heard that he or she had done something that seemed insensitive to you, or that implied that you were not that important to him or her. Recall how your friend reacted defensively and then how the conflict escalated.

- Why do you think you became defensive?
- Think of how you might have remained open and engaged when you approached your friend with your perceptions about his or her behavior toward you.
- Imagine how he or she might have responded differently.

Think of a time when your friend or partner approached you in a defensive manner and you reacted by being defensive yourself.

- Think of how you might have inhibited your defensive tendency and responded in an open and engaged manner.
- How do you think the subsequent conversation would have evolved differently?

Recall a recent time when you were open and engaged with your partner. Remember that when you are engaged, you are as open to your partner's experience as to your own (this is intersubjectivity). When thinking about that time or other recent similar times, reflect on the experience with regard to whether it contained features of the following:

- Playfulness
- Acceptance
- Curiosity
- Empathy

Think of a difference that you have with your partner that you tend to avoid for fear it will cause a bigger conflict. Think of approaching your partner to discuss it without being defensive. Reflect on PACE and consider if features of that attitude might help you to address the difference more productively. Try to stay open and engaged with PACE when you approach your partner. Later, reflect on whether or not this attitude was helpful.

Finally, I should mention seven mental activities that have been found both to facilitate the functioning of the brain and to help create a balanced life, thus optimizing our engagement in healthy relationships. Participating in these activities on a daily basis is likely to help you develop the mental, physical, and relational skills that are important to you.

The Healthy Mind Platter: Seven daily essential mental activities to optimize brain matter and create well-being[4]

Focus Time	When we closely focus on tasks in a goal-oriented way, we take on challenges that make deep connections in the brain.
Playtime	When we allow ourselves to be spontaneous or creative, playfully enjoying novel experiences, we help make new connections in the brain.
Connecting Time	When we connect with other people, ideally in person, and when we take time to appreciate our connection to the natural world around us, we activate and reinforce the brain's relational circuitry.
Physical Time	When we move our bodies, aerobically if medically possible, we strengthen the brain in many ways.
Time-in	When we quietly reflect internally, focusing on sensations, images, feelings, and thoughts, we help to better integrate the brain.

| Downtime | When we are non-focused, without any specific goal, and let our mind wander or simply relax, we help the brain recharge. |
| Sleep Time | When we give the brain the rest it needs, we consolidate learning and recover from the experiences of the day. |

KEY 4

BUILD YOUR
REFLECTIVE CAPACITY

In this chapter and the next I will be focusing on two central human capacities—thinking and feeling—that complement each other. *Reflective functioning* represents the thinking dimension of your mind and focuses on your inner life—your thoughts, emotions, wishes, memories, intentions, perceptions, values, and beliefs—as well as the inner lives of others.

Reflective functioning is *what* our minds consider; *emotional functioning*, on the other hand, is *how* our minds consider it. Your emotional functioning is reflected by your decision to either approach or avoid, enjoy or not enjoy a conversation with someone. Indeed, the intensity and complexity of all our desires are part of our emotional functioning. Our emotions might be broadly seen as positive or negative, pleasurable or painful, though there are many variations along the range of these two states, sometimes they are mixed together, and they may be regulated or dysregulated. Your emotional capacity is enhanced by your reflective capacity and vice versa. When they are integrated into your day-to-day functioning, your relationships are more likely to be healthy.

For example, your awareness that you are sad because your friend did not want to go to a movie with you is an instance of your reflective functioning. Suppose you are also aware that your sadness is more acute than you would have anticipated and also has a component of fear. You become aware that it was acute because your friend has declined your invitations to do things together a number of times and you are afraid that your friend may not enjoy being with you so much anymore.

Your emotional functioning refers to your sadness itself, as well as its intensity and the associated quality of fear of loss of the relationship. Your emotions convey your experience of the event (your friend's declining your invitation). They represent your first assessment of whether the event is something you desire. If our emotions are intense, frequent, or both, they are informing us that we should reflect on the event more deeply to understand its meaning for us. This enables us to better discuss an event with our partner in order to further enhance our relationship.

This chapter focuses on the characteristics of your reflective functioning, while the next looks at your emotional functioning. Given the value of their integration, there will necessarily be overlap between this chapter and the next.

Reflecting on Relationships in General

First I will take an overview of relationships with a wide-angle lens, to discern patterns and preferences. There is value in reflecting on what we want in relationships, whether these be with acquaintances, friends, our children, or our partner. Being aware of what we are looking for in a friendship once we get to know someone guides us in deciding what sort of person we would be most satisfied with having as a friend. When we mindfully and actively develop a friendship, all the while maintaining a clear idea of what we were hoping for, we foster success. Friendships that develop out of circumstances, convenience, or necessity are more likely to fail—or to require significant boundaries or compromises if they are to persist—than are friendships that we have reflected on and actively chosen.

What Do Relationships Mean to Me?

The first area to be aware of involves what we hope for in our relationships. How important are they in our lives, what role do they play in our attainment of our goals in life, and in what parts of our lives are they particularly valuable? The following are some questions to ask about what you want in your relationships:

Do you want a balance between safety and adventure or one more than the other?

Do you want a relationship centered on discussing practical matters, sharing emotional experiences, or a balance of both?

Do you want a relationship that allows for separate interests, stresses common interests, or provides a balance between the two?

Do you want a relationship with someone who is strongly self-reliant, who relies on you heavily, or whose degree of reliance is somewhere in between?

Do you want a relationship with someone who enjoys conversation, prefers silence, or lies in the middle of the spectrum?

Do you want a relationship with someone who expresses affection openly and often or who prefers to be more muted?

Do you want a relationship with someone who easily divulges his or her inner life, is more reserved, or lies somewhere in between?

Do you want a relationship with someone who is relaxed and laid back, who is an active, high-achieving type, or who lies somewhere in between?

What Am I Like in Relationships?

Once we assess what our preferred relationship would be, it is important to know how we function in our relationships. What are our strengths and weaknesses? How open and engaged are we and how likely are we to acknowledge to ourselves and others that we have made a mistake? Reflecting on our weaknesses is not the easiest thing to do, but we must examine them if we are to do our part in avoiding conflicts and repairing our relationships after conflicts do arise. If we cannot acknowledge our own mistakes and challenges we may very well become defensive whenever the other person expresses dissatisfaction with something that occurs in the relationship. The following questions are useful in this regard:

Do I make sacrifices for the benefit of my friend or partner or am I willing to help only when it is convenient for me?

Am I willing to admit that I contributed to a conflict or do I generally blame my friend or partner?

Am I as comfortable relying on my friend or partner as I am with him or her relying on me?

Do I become possessive and jealous?

When I am disappointed in something that my friend or partner has done, do I assume that he or she was impelled by the worst motive and react accordingly, do I assume that there was a good reason for the action I didn't like and overlook it, or do I try to avoid making any assumptions but instead wait to ask my friend or partner what he or she did?

Do I try to understand the world my friend or partner inhabits and do I care as much about what happens to him or her as I do when it comes to my own circumstances?

Do I avoid conflicts for fear they will hurt the relationship or do I address them directly with the aim of improving the relationship?

Do I have expectations of my friend or partner that I have never communicated and then get annoyed when he or she does not meet them?

Do I assume that since I like something, my friend or partner will like it too and then get annoyed when he or she does not?

How Do I Reflect on Others?

One last point: It is important to be aware of how deeply we try to get to know the person with whom we are having a relationship. Do we put a great deal of effort into trying to understand what is unique about our friend or partner's inner life and try not to react to his or her behavior until we first gain insight into the thoughts, feelings, and motives that led to the behavior? Here are some questions to consider:

Do I notice nonverbal expressions that might suggest what my friend or partner is thinking, feeling, or planning to do?

Do I ask the opinion of my friend or partner about whether my guesses about his or her inner life are accurate?

Do I assume that I know why he or she did something, without asking for confirmation?

Do I value getting to know him or her from the inside out?

Am I interested when my friend or partner relates what he or she thinks and feels and what his or her dreams are about?

Do I ask my friend or partner about his or her thoughts, feelings, and intentions, both in the immediate moment and in general, and am I interested in his or her responses?

Example

Edward is often attracted to ambitious, energetic women willing to put in long hours at work. These women are independent minded, relying on their own abilities and taking the initiative rather than turning to others for assistance. The women who appeal to him openly express their desire to be with him, are assertive, and are not inhibited about sharing their feelings, ideas, and wishes.

While Edward is consistently attracted to this type of woman, he also seems to easily become frustrated and dissatisfied with his relationship. He begins to feel that she is a bit too selfish for him. She seems to be unwilling to compromise on how much time they spend together and on how they'll spend their time. He begins to think she is not very affectionate and that he is just not that special to her.

If Edward does not reflect too deeply on what he truly wants in his relationships or on what he contributes to the problems that begin to emerge in them, he may be more responsible for the causes of his subsequent frustration about the relationships than the women are. While on the surface he might seem to simply want to be with a strong and independent woman, at a deeper level the reason for this may be that he fears being with a woman who relies on him and has expectations of him, worried that she will be what he considers dependent. He may in part be attracted to a woman's trait of independence because he can then depend upon her, but he is unable to acknowledge his dependent traits, not wanting to feel that he is dependent, that is, weak and inadequate. In essence, Edward may want to be with an independent woman who centers her life around him, giving him a sense that she values his strength and competence and worth to the extent that she would want to give up everything for him. Then he could lead an independent life on the outside while secretly depending on her on the inside. No wonder Edward often becomes dissatisfied in his relationships. He is not likely to find such an independent woman who seems to depend on him—giving up a lot for him—without being a burden to him and at the same time allowing him to depend on her, while pretending that he doesn't.

If Edward could reflect on who he is he might discover that he does want to be able to emotionally rely on a partner who also will rely on him. He might acknowledge that he wants safety and a comfortable home life more than he wants a high degree of achievement either for himself or his partner. Knowing that about himself, he might seek a woman who seems to share his goals for a relationship. He also might be more direct in communicating this to women he meets and then attract the interest of a woman who is aware of wanting similar things in her relationship with a partner.

Reflecting on This Specific Relationship

It is equally important to reflect on each relationship that is important to us. We need to ask how the unique qualities of an individual with whom we are in a relationship match what is important to us in relationships in general. If the unique qualities of a particular relationship are different from those of our usual relationships, how did this relationship develop and why do we remain in it? Here are some questions to ask:

What do I like/not like about this relationship?
Why do I act the way I do and say the things I do in this relationship?

How important is this person to me? Why is the person that important?

Is this person similar/different from people in my other important
relationships?

Will these similarities/differences make the relationship more satisfying or more challenging or both?

How important is it to me to maintain this relationship at this level?
How committed am I to it?

How important is it to me to deepen this relationship and increase
my commitment?

What does this person think of our relationship?

What feelings does he or she associate with our relationship?

What does he or she want in our relationship?

Example

Darlene's childhood was as close to ideal as she could imagine.
Her parents were both successful professionals as well as actively
engaged with their three children. Darlene never wanted for love,
support, or guidance. Now she was on the faculty of an excellent
university and had every reason to anticipate that her life as an
adult would approximate that of her parents. To find a partner with
whom to share a home and maybe start a family was her last important unmet goal.

Darlene met and dated a number of men she found pleasing,
some from her university and some working in professions similar
to those of her parents. In the main, these men had much in common with her, including a desire for the kind of life she wanted. A
few seemed ideal, but she hesitated. They were caring and sensitive men, successful and supportive of her career. Why would she
hesitate? Was she being too selective, seeking the perfect partner?

Then one day she met Gavin. He seemed different, though
Darlene could not say how. He most likely would not have the
same level of success as some of the other men. He was a high
school teacher and saw himself in that job his whole life. He did
not seem to be any more sensitive or caring or supportive than the

other men. He might even have a few more small, frustrating habits than they did. So why was she so attracted to him? She wondered and reflected. Being a professor, she did not have confidence in trusting her gut instinct.

One Sunday evening after she and Gavin had spent a nice afternoon at her parents' home, she knew. When she was with him, he expressed, and she felt, the same degree of relaxed warmth that was characteristic of her parents' relationship. It felt so appealing and comfortable — being with him reminded her of how her parents were with each other. Not that his personality was like her father's; nor was hers like her mother's. No, it was something more subtle and encompassing. Her parents were able to be themselves when they were together, with a sense of complete acceptance, without having to hide what they thought and felt. She wanted that in her relationship with a partner someday. She had vaguely been aware of it, and now, having met Gavin, she had no doubts.

Darlene had a habit of reflecting on her inner life while being aware of and often successfully making sense of the inner lives of her friends. Had she not reflected on her experience with men, she might well have chosen a man to be her partner who had many of the characteristics she wanted. Or she might have noticed that he did not quite have the relaxed warmth that she liked but then convinced herself that such a quality was not that important anyway. She might have decided that the first man who demonstrated success, sensitivity, and support for her career would do. Or that Gavin could not be the right man because his level of financial success was not as high as she might have liked. Those were important traits in choosing a man. But Darlene's hesitation demonstrated the importance that she gave to reflecting on her choices and making sense of them.

Reflecting on Self and Other in the Present Moment

The building blocks of every relationship and of our goals for our relationships in general are day-to-day, moment-to-moment interactions and their effects on us in the present moment. Our relationships are more meaningful and satisfying when we are fully present with the other and aware of what is happening within ourselves and what we sense is happening within the other. When we are open and engaged with the other, rather than being preoccupied with other things or taking the other for granted, the relationship is more likely to develop and conflicts and misunderstandings are less likely to occur. Relationships begin to lose meaning when we become less aware of the other in the present moment and begin to relate to our partner mostly through habits and assumptions that we developed in the early stages of the relationship. The following questions might help to maintain the vitality and deepening nature of our relationships:

What am I thinking and feeling now with the other person?
What are my motives for doing what I am doing?
What is my partner thinking and feeling?
What are the motives behind what he or she is doing?
What part did I play in the conflict we just had?
Do we both want to do what we are now doing? If not, why are we doing it?
If he or she says one thing and seems to want something different, do I comment on it or not? If not, why not?
Am I or are we bored together today? Is this a pattern developing that we might address?
Am I dissatisfied with something about my partner? If so, why? Is this something that needs to be addressed if the relationship is important and if I want it to remain so?
Did I enjoy my time with my partner? Did I tell him or her? If not, why not?

Example

Matt and Linda had been living together for two years but were finding that the romance was fading and that things were not nearly as exciting and enjoyable as they once were. They often felt dissatisfied when they were together but did not know why.

LINDA: Hey, since we both have some free time this afternoon, do you want to take the canoe out to the lake for a few hours? Maybe make a lunch to take with us?

MATT: I'd rather not today. I'm planning to go over to Harry's and help him with a project he's working on. He mentioned the other day that he hoped to work on it this weekend and he's really behind on it. I told him I'd stop by and give him a hand.

LINDA: Help him another time! Lately there haven't been many times when we were both free at the same time.

In this scenario, Linda urges Matt to change his mind and then gives him a reason. If she had simply expressed her wish to spend more time with him when they were both free, in the near future, he might have been more open to her request to be together more. Or if she had articulated that she wanted them to find a way to spend time together that afternoon after Matt spent time with his friend, he might have responded positively. Instead he is abrupt:

MATT: No thanks, Linda. I told Harry that I'd give him a hand.

Matt's quick comment that his plans were not open for discussion, without acknowledging Linda's wish that they spend more time together, may have been triggered by her immediate request to change his mind. Still, if he had acknowledged her wish by saying that he too would like to spend some time with her, but that it was important that he first help Harry for a few hours, she might have responded positively. Her response reflects her negative reaction:

LINDA: I have the feeling that Harry is more important to you than I am.

Linda takes to another level the mild frustration they both seem to feel at this point. She assumes that Matt's motive for helping Harry is Matt's preference for Harry; Harry is more important to Matt than she is. Matt's decision to help Harry is for Linda a metaphor for their damaged relationship. She expresses her assumptions through anger, which makes her comment even more difficult for Matt to respond to with openness. He responds defensively to Linda's strong assumption about the motives for his behavior:

MATT: Where did that come from? I made a commitment to him. And besides, I just want to spend a few hours with him!

LINDA: Rather than a few hours with me!

MATT: This has nothing to do with you, Linda! Why are you taking it so personally?

Now both Matt and Linda are extremely defensive. Neither is making an honest effort to understand the other. Linda is giving great importance to Matt's not spending a few hours with her, and Matt's question about why she takes his behavior "personally" comes from his annoyance and will certainly not lead to an open discussion of their conflict. This is apparent from Linda's response, as she further enlarges the significance of Matt's plan to help his friend:

LINDA: You always have some reason for not doing something nice with me! Today it's Harry! Tomorrow, who knows? You'll find something!

Matt again has a defensive response, reacting to Linda's global criticism of him and his motives:

MATT: That's not fair! We spent the weekend together up in the mountains a few weeks ago!

LINDA: And how selfish I am to want to spend time with you more than once a month!

MATT: You're making a lot out of this one afternoon!

LINDA: And you're showing me a lot by not wanting to go canoeing with me!

MATT: Make of it what you want, Linda! You always do anyway!

Linda continues to assume that there are negative motives behind Matt's choice to spend a few hours with his friend. Matt's defensive response now becomes more similar to Linda's in that he expresses a global generalization ("You always do anyway!") about Linda's judging his motives that she assumes to be present.

LINDA: Nice, Matt, so this is all my fault!
MATT: Well, its not mine! *(Linda leaves the room in anger. Matt finishes his breakfast in anger. Both question why they have never noticed how selfish the other one really is.)*

The conflict has become an either/or proposition with all the responsibility being placed on the other person. Each is likely to believe that the other person started the argument. Many of us may say that Linda started it. Matt experienced her controlling stance and did not notice her underlying fear that their spending less time together meant that she was less important to him. His defensive response is understandable, though if he had been able to remain open and engaged with her, they might have been able to address her underlying worries. If Linda had been more reflective about her fears and doubts about Matt's experience of the relationship, she might have addressed them with him in an open and engaged manner. The goal here is not to find someone to blame for starting the argument but rather to be aware of opportunities for both parties to reflect on what is happening early enough in the interaction to resolve the conflict when it would be easier to do so. Neither is likely to see that regardless of who started it, both quickly became embroiled in the pattern of defense of oneself and blame of the other for a conflict that was deepening as they spoke.

Now let's revisit this exchange between Matt and Linda. In this instance, Linda manages her initial disappointment without becoming defensive.

LINDA: Hey, since we both have some free time this afternoon, do you want to take the canoe out to the lake for a few hours? Maybe make a lunch to take with us?

MATT: I'd rather not today. I'm planning to go over to Harry's and help him with a project he's working on. He mentioned the other day that he hoped to work on it this weekend and he's really behind on it. I told him I'd stop by and give him a hand.

LINDA: That's too bad. Lately there haven't been many times when we're both free at the same time. How about when you're at Harry's I'll get dinner ready? When you get back we can eat and then if you're not too tired, maybe go for a moonlight walk down by the river.

MATT: That would be nice! I can't imagine being too tired for that, especially since "moonlight walk" means to me that we'll be walking slowly.

LINDA: You got it. As slow as you want. The moon will be rising slowly anyway and the river will always be there.

In this dialogue Linda curbs her disappointment so she doesn't become annoyed and tell Matt what to do. She then communicates her wish to do something with him, after first accepting his plan to help his friend. Her readiness to prepare dinner while he is at Harry's and her suggestion of a romantic time together afterward leads Matt to easily agree to the plan.

Let's revisit the dialogue a second time. This time Matt is able to inhibit his defensive response and remain open to helping Linda with her annoyance, without agreeing to what she is expecting of him.

LINDA: Hey, since we both have some free time this afternoon, do you want to take the canoe out to the lake for a few hours? Maybe make a lunch to take with us?

MATT: I'd rather not today. I'm planning to go over to Harry's and help him with a project he's working on. He mentioned the other day that he hoped to work on it this weekend and he's really behind on it. I told him I'd stop by and give him a hand.

LINDA: Help him another time! Lately there haven't been many times when we're both free at the same time.

MATT: I hadn't thought of that, Linda, but I think you're right. We haven't been able to spend much time with each other in the past few weeks.

LINDA: So how about calling Harry and suggesting another day?

Matt's ability to not become defensive in response to Linda's telling him what she wants him to do, along with his positive response to her wish that they spend more time together, enables Linda to express her wish as a request, not a command.

MATT: I'd enjoy the canoe ride too, Linda, but I feel that I should help Harry out like I told him I would. What do you think about us doing something this evening after dinner?

LINDA: That would work for me. Maybe I could get the dinner started while you're at Harry's.

Again, with Matt's taking the lead in remaining open and engaged and not being defensive, Linda is able to follow him with a joint desire to find time together while Matt maintains his wish to help his friend.

In this case, one member of the relationship becomes defensive, and the other member inhibits a natural tendency to become defensive in return, enabling the first member to move out of the defensive stance and become open and engaged. If Linda seldom becomes defensive, then Matt might simply reflect that she was having a hard day and not address it later. If Linda habitually reacts defensively when she is disappointed, then most likely it would be wise for Matt to address that with her so that he is not the one who is always responsible for preventing an escalation in the conflicts in their relationship.

MATT: Or you could go to Harry's with me and help him too so I'd get done earlier. *(Smiles.)*

LINDA: How about I stay here and make dinner? *(Also smiles.)*

When one member of a relationship is able to remain reflective during an interaction with the other, early disagreements often do not escalate. When both are reflective, early disagreements are seen as normal aspects of all relationships and are simply accepted and handled. When neither partner is reflective, routine disagreements often are the beginning stages of intensifying relationship conflicts and the eventual breakdown of the relationship.

In short, with reflective functioning, we do not react to the behavior (whether spoken words or actions) without first addressing it, making sense of it, and then responding to it in a way that is congruent with its meaning. If the behavior represents a difference or conflict, it can be addressed in a more successful manner than if we did not first make sense of it. If the behavior represents something different that is not a problem for us, it is often simply clarified and then accepted.

Exercises

Think about an important relationship in your life. Reflect on your thoughts, feelings, wishes, intentions, and perceptions regarding this particular relationship. Now reflect on what your friend or partner might think, feel, wish, intend, and perceive about his or her relationship with you. Compare the similarities and differences between how you experience the relationship and how you think your friend or partner does. Given the nature of the relationship, is there value in increasing the similarities and decreasing the differences? If so, how do you think that you might approach that?

Reflect on recent (within the past year) events of the types listed below. When you consider your thoughts, feelings, perceptions, and intentions at the time, reflect on how the event may have turned out differently if you had reflected differently.

- A conflict with your friend or partner
- An experience of increased distance between you and your friend or partner

- An enjoyable event with your friend or partner
- An experience of deep sharing or comfort with your friend or partner

Consider your relationship with your mother or father, with the knowledge that reflecting on important past relationships can change your experience and memory of those relationships, and do the following:

1. Write a letter (with no intention of sharing it) to your parent that includes your past thoughts, feelings, wishes, and memories about your parent and your relationship with your parent.
2. Write a letter that represents what you *believe* would be your parent's response to your letter. This would include your parent's thoughts, feelings, wishes, intentions, and memories about you and your parent's relationship with you.
3. Write a letter that represents what you *wish* was your parent's response to your letter.

Reflect on yourself and your relationships in ways that are likely to be unique to you and that could never be covered in a book. What makes you and your relationships unique? With regard to your relationships, what are your unique wishes? Challenges? Sources of joy? Are there areas of pride regarding who you are in relationships? Are there areas of doubt? After so reflecting, where are you? Is this where you want to be? If not, why not? If not, what plans might you develop for getting there?

BUILD YOUR
EMOTIONAL COMPETENCE

Ann Marie was in her second month at the clinic where she worked as a speech therapist when she started to spend some of her free time with Brenda, an occupational therapist. They had a lot in common and enjoyed their lunches together. She envisioned Brenda as a friend to get together with once in a while on weekends. If only Brenda didn't like Christine so much! Ann Marie didn't see what she saw in her. Christine seemed shallow and moody and too into drama. It didn't really matter though; she and Brenda were just friends.

As the months went on Ann Marie liked spending more and more time with Brenda. Ann Marie felt safe with her, they had a lot of fun together, they helped each other through the frustrations of work and going out with guys, and they exchanged little gifts. As these positive experiences and related emotions increased, so too did some distressing ones. Ann Marie would often feel disappointed when Brenda had commitments with others, or when she was withdrawn or irritable. She became a bit jealous when Brenda mentioned that she and Christine had made plans to do something together. She became angry when Brenda did not remember her birthday. She was hurt when Brenda didn't seem interested when she told her about how worried she was about her sister's divorce.

As relationships develop, they are tinged with more and more emotions. Great! Emotions add vitality to our lives. Emotions give energy to our thoughts and actions. However, just as relationships engender enjoyable emotions, they create stressful ones. Qualities that we like about a relationship tend to have parallel qualities that we do not like. We like that we spend time with a person, but we don't like that there are times when we are not together. We like when our friend is interested in a story we're telling, but we don't like it when our friend does not appear to be interested in our story. We like knowing that we can rely on someone in some things, we don't like that we can't rely on the same person for other things. As sharing what we have in common becomes more enjoyable to us, conflicts become more stressful. The more important the relationship becomes, the more intense are the emotions—both positive and negative—associated with it. If we want to avoid intense relationships, we might choose to avoid having important relationships. Of course, we might then find ourselves struggling with emotions associated with loneliness.

It is relevant here to consider that the word *mind* refers to the flow of energy and information in our brain. (This clear, succinct, definition of *mind* is presented by Dan Siegel in many of his writings, including *The Developing Mind,* referred to earlier.) Our reflective functioning represents an important component of the information in our mind, while our emotions represent the *energy* of our mind. Remember from the previous chapter, reflective functioning is *what* our minds consider, and emotional functioning is *how* our minds consider it. Our relationships function best when they have a balance between our reflective functioning and our emotions. As a particular relationship becomes more important to us it manifests more intense and varied emotions. These emotions make our relationships more meaningful to us; as a result they produce warmth and joy when they are developing and fear and grief when they are ending.

As a relationship becomes more embedded in our emotional life, it needs to be equally embedded in our reflective life, if it is to remain healthy. For our emotions to remain regulated they need to be integrated with our reflective functioning. Strong, lasting, meaningful relationships contain an equal balance of comprehensive, well-functioning emotions and reflection. In this chapter I will focus on our emotional life and how the development of this aspect of our mind is crucial if we are to maintain healthy relationships.

Our Emotions

In years past neurologists spoke of the emotional part of the brain (such as the limbic system) and the cognitive part (the cortex). Neuropsychologists and neurobiologists no longer speak in such simplistic terms in describing the very complex functioning of the brain. Now their research supports the belief that our emotions permeate every cell and circuit of the brain. We used to be told that we should rely on our reasoning to guide our behavior. We had to develop our reasoning abilities to know what was best for us. But our reasoning abilities were also seen as crucial in the suppression of our impulsive emotions. We were told that if we followed our emotions, inevitably we would be led astray. We needed to inhibit our emotions—through reasoning and its "enforcer," *will power*—and then turn to reason to select our goals and the means of attaining them. But there is a problem with all this: Our brains don't work that way!

   Horrible decisions may occur when we try to rely exclusively on logic and reason to make the important choices and decisions in our lives. What is "best" for us is not often the choice that finishes at the top of the pro and con lists we obsessively develop. The difficulty with having confidence in such lists is that the components are based on our values, desires, judgments, preferences, beliefs, thoughts, feelings, and histories and none of these can be defined with any objective measure. The amount of weight we give to any factor on the lists is based on these subjective personal states. What proves to be best for us does not derive from isolated reason but rather from our intuition, our *felt sense*, our *gut sense*, and our imagination. These dimensions that lead to our sense of what is best originate in the areas of the brain that are the most integrative, using awareness that emerges from our reflecting thoughts and emotions, along with input from our heart, lungs, and gut (in scientific terms, the ventral vagal circuit of the autonomic nervous system). This deeply subjective, integrative knowledge emerges in the brain from the anterior cingulate cortex, the insula, the hippocampus, the nucleus accumbens, and the amygdala; and it—especially when such knowledge concerns relationships—also involves our sense of the experience of the other person. The brain supplies us with this source of knowledge through the social engagement system and other related neurological circuits.

When our emotions have developed well and when they are integrated with our reflective functioning and the sources of our knowledge of our body, they often are at the forefront of our awareness about what is best for us. Sometimes what is pleasurable is best and what is not pleasurable is not in our best interest, while at other times it is the opposite; a short-term pleasure leads to long-term problems. There are also many shades of gray and at times it is hard to know if a person is desirable or not. You may feel mixed emotions or ambivalence toward a person. We have a multitude of emotions, sometimes at odds with one another and sometimes supporting one another. So let's look at our emotions—especially those that most closely relate to relationships—both alone and in groupings, and let's look at how those emotions can best facilitate healthy relationships.

Your emotions are classified as either positive or negative, although such a system is not nearly as straightforward as it might look when an event contains both positive and negative emotions.

Relationships and Positive Emotions

We are a social species. Many scientists now believe that our brain is designed more for altruism than for selfishness, more for cooperation than for competition—at least when we're feeling safe! Since attachment functions in part to develop your safety it is not surprising that healthy relationships are experienced as loving relationships that are associated with many positive emotions: affection, passion, joy, comfort, gratitude, excitement, pleasure. These emotions bring color to days that would otherwise be gray. They carry vitality and momentum, when without them we might become listless and bored.

Love

It is hard to imagine having a healthy relationship without there being the ingredient of love. You might restrict the use of the word *love* to only your partner and immediate family. You might also use it in speaking of your good friends or even close colleagues. Given this broader perspective on the word, it might be regarded as having the following components:

- You believe the life and well-being of your friend to be as important as your own.
- You deeply enjoy being with your friend, sharing a variety of experiences and ideas.
- You are interested in knowing more and more about your friend.
- You turn to your friend for comfort and support and you provide similar emotional strength for him or her when he or she is in need.
- You are committed to resolving difficulties that are present that might hurt the relationship.
- Your interactions are reciprocal.

When you love someone you want to be near the person and have feelings of warmth and affection associated with him or her and your relationship. Various neurological transmitters are associated with love; among them are oxytocin, estrogen, prolactin, and vasopressin. You are likely to be healthier and to live longer when you experience love in relationship with others. Your immune system prefers love to isolation.

Enjoyment

You might say that the more you love a person the more *enjoyment* is present in your relationship. It is hard to imagine being in love with a person and not enjoying being with him or her. When you are with a person you like your brain transmits dopamine, which generates the feeling of pleasure. Dopamine is also often generated in the brain through the use of drugs. In fact, if you do not experience much pleasure in your relationships, you are at a greater risk for substance abuse and other addictions (gambling, sex). In experiments with rats, it was found that the mothers prefer nursing their babies to accepting cocaine, whereas after their infants are weaned, they are much more likely to choose cocaine.

When enjoyment in your relationship is high, you are likely to have few doubts about it and you may take the enjoyment for granted. As enjoyment gradually decreases you may not even notice that it is diminishing, as contentment is a product of familiarity and habit. You might be devoting less time to your relationship and not doing the activities together that you used to do that generated the greatest enjoyment. With less enjoyment you do fewer joint activities, generating less enjoyment still. Better to work to maintain enjoyment in your relationships just as you work to maintain your physical well-being through exercise. Enjoyment doesn't just happen, at least not after the honeymoon is over. You need to reflect on it, identify what you enjoy the most in your time with your partner and commit to ensuring that you have the time to do what you have identified. Of course part of your enjoyment will come from the enjoyment that you bring to your partner. (This is the case in all relationships—they exist best when they are reciprocal.)

If enjoyment in your relationship is low you might first give thought to the overall place of enjoyment in your life. Do you stress achievement to such an extent that you leave little room for enjoyment? Do you stress impressing others, having a spotless home, or preparing for the future to such an extent that you devalue ensuring that your life in the present contains enjoyment? If so, reflect on why preparation for living, for avoiding trouble, or for keeping up with the Joneses is so important to you. A sense that you are only worthwhile if you are successful? That you must avoid failure or mistakes or disapproval at all costs? Does it come from scarcity, whether financial, psychological, or relational?

If enjoyment is generally a low priority, reflect on giving it a more prominent place in your life. Set aside hours and days where there are no goals other than to participate in life with enjoyment. Reflect on the sources of deepest joy for you and create room for those sources of joy and even see if you can further expand the joy that they offer you.

You may struggle if your enjoyment in your relationship is high but your friend's or partner's enjoyment seems low. This is likely to lead to insecurity on your part and doubts that the relationship will last. In the example given above concerning Ann Marie and Brenda, Ann Marie began to lose confidence that Brenda experienced the same degree of enjoyment in being together as she did. This engendered in Ann Marie the negative emotions of disappointment, anger, and jealousy with regard to this relationship.

Since this book is about healthy relationships, give some thought also to how to increase your interpersonal enjoyments. Many positive experiences are enjoyed more — traveling, attending a movie or musical, eating out or exploring a nearby park — when shared with someone who is important to you. The enjoyment felt in shared learning, discoveries, and accomplishments is often more than double that felt when doing them alone. Simply experiencing your partner's enjoyment adds a dimension to your own that is not available in any other manner.

Commitment

Even when you protect and nurture your times of enjoyment with your partner, they will not always be present. That's where *commit-*

ment is needed. (Commitment might not be regarded by some as an emotion, but it certainly is associated with positive features of relationships and will be discussed here.) During the difficult times, the somewhat boring times, the conflicts and separations—realities that are periodically present in all relationships—commitment generates safety through the knowledge that the relationship will remain, regardless of present strife. Commitment takes you through the ups and downs, through better or worse, in the knowledge that your love is not dependent on constant enjoyment.

Commitment requires that you step out of the immediate conflict or sense of distance and discord and remember your positive past experiences and your anticipated future ones. Commitment reminds you of what you love in your partner so that your relationship is experienced as bigger than your conflicts. Commitment keeps you grounded in the knowledge that a relationship without the down times and the hurt feelings does not exist. Commitment reminds you too that when you get through the hard times together you both will be stronger because of your efforts, and your relationship will be as well.

Passion

Your relationship is also likely to contain *passion*. This will often be present during times of sexuality and romance but it may be present at other times as well, when feelings of love are intense or when they take you by surprise in response to a gaze, a gesture, a flower, or a clean sink. Sometimes with your partner you may acutely sense how lucky you are and maybe how lucky you both are to be carried along by your unique experience of love.

Your passion for your partner is also probably evident in your intense feelings of concern and protectiveness when it comes to the overall well-being of your partner (and clearly of your child as well). You will not hesitate to place your partner's well-being above your own and feel intense emotions that are congruent with your partner's highs and lows. Your partner's life is experienced as deeply as is your own. That is passion.

Gratitude

Sometimes in those unexpected moments, you may also experi-ence *gratitude* toward your friend or partner after he or she has done something considerate and been generous toward you or pro-vided you with comfort and support. Or your partner may have given you a meaningful gift that demonstrates how he or she thinks of you when you are not together. Or you may feel gratitude simply when you are aware of how often the gift of that person is there for you, no matter what you are doing.

Gratitude is a warm and comfortable emotion that demon-strates that you are aware of how important your partner is to you and your life. When you notice that your partner also experiences gratitude for having you in his or her life, you are likely to feel even more elated. You may well experience yourself as you deeply want to be, when you experience your partner's gratitude.

Loving and Being Loved:
The Ultimate in Reciprocity

You may think you just want someone who will love you and then you'll be happy. If so, you may be wrong. You also may want some-one who will want and accept your love in return. Being loved, without having the opportunity to love in return, will make your relationship unstable over time. Your partner will tire of loving you without being loved in return and you will tire of being loved without having your love sought after and valued. People who love but are not comfortable being loved are likely to not be com-fortable relying on someone else. They may feel vulnerable know-ing that if they seek out and enjoy being loved, and then lose the relationship, it will be very painful. People who want to be loved but are not comfortable loving may have little confidence that they have something to offer their partner and that if they actively love someone their love will be rejected. They may also prefer be-ing loved because they feel dependent in their relationship and their partner's love makes them feel cared for as if they were a child again.

You may notice that in some relationships one person assumes a more parental role and the other person functions more like a child. The one person is comfortable loving and communicating love and the other is comfortable with the experience of being loved. For a time, possibly years, this might work well for this couple. Once in a while the one person might miss being loved and the other misses having his or her love happily received. And he or she may become annoyed with the other as the months or years go by. Adults, through integrating years of new experiences and other relationships, tend to change. One or the other—the one in the parent role or in the child role—is likely to become dissatisfied with this role and seek a more reciprocal relationship. When both people in the couple become dissatisfied around the same time, they may be able to transition into a relationship that is more reciprocal. Now, both are comfortable with both loving and being loved, giving and receiving, comforting and being comforted, talking and listening. Now there is more reciprocal sharing and turn-taking among equals. Such characterizes the healthiest relationships.

Relationships and Negative Emotions

We would like it if relationships involved only positive emotions, never negative ones. Sometimes we try very hard to make that true and allow ourselves to see only the positive facets of our relationships, hoping that the negative ones will fade away. When we ignore negative emotions, though, they tend to lurk in the background, appearing all of a sudden and much more intensely. A better choice is to address our negative emotions, understand them, and express them in ways that improve our relationships rather than harm them. I will now consider the most common emotions that present challenges for healthy relationships.

Shame and Guilt

For years psychologists did not agree on the differences between shame and guilt and the two terms were often used interchangeably. No wonder we often confuse the two as well and in so doing misunderstand the important differences between shame and guilt and the implications of these differences for healthy relationships. First, consider them separately:

Shame

- Present in infants/toddlers. Precedes guilt developmentally. When shame is kept small and the relationship repaired, there is room for guilt to develop.
- Experienced as your sense of self, a global sense of who you are.
- Gives a sense of being bad, worthless, hopeless, unlovable.
- Entails a focus on your self; little awareness of the other person.
- Motivates you to hide from the "truth"; plays a part in lying, minimizing, blaming, making excuses, and becoming enraged when hiding is impossible.
- Entails pervasive, intense pain when experienced. Tends to be lasting. Engenders strategies, noted above, to prevent the pain.
- Interferes with development of guilt; interferes with the awareness of empathy, which is central in experiencing guilt.

Guilt

- Develops and becomes organized between two and three years of age when not hampered in its development by a pervasive sense of shame.
- Emotion specific to your behavior. Associated with emotions of remorse, regret.
- Fosters a sense that your behavior was wrong/mistaken.
- Involves a focus on the other person and how your behavior affected him or her.

- Motivates you to acknowledge what you did, apologize, and repair the relationship through subsequent behaviors.
- Causes milder pain than that of shame; tends to decrease or end when the relationship is repaired.

The presence of chronic shame can make it difficult for you to develop a healthy relationship, whereas guilt should promote a healthy relationship. You might even say that the function of guilt is to protect the relationship, while the function of shame is to protect the self. All relationships involve problems, mistakes, misunderstandings, and conflicts. The emotion of guilt makes you aware of how your behavior may have hurt your partner and the relationship itself. The pain of guilt tends to be mild enough to signal to you that you may have caused pain to your partner and it motivates you to repair the pain that you caused. Your guilt and the subsequent changes in your behavior are likely to build confidence in your friend or partner that you are committed to him or her and to your relationship. Your partner knows you have accepted responsibility for your mistake and the pain that you caused and he or she is more likely to trust you and your commitment to the relationship.

Shame, by contrast, is associated with your sense of yourself, separate from your partner and the relationship. Shame is such a painful emotion that it is not long before the child or young adult has created elaborate defenses against experiencing shame. Often lying is a shame-based activity. The strength of your shame can be so great that you lie to yourself. To avoid the anguish of shame you may refuse to acknowledge what you did may have hurt your relationship with your friend.

Thus, realistic guilt may be a gift to your relationships, while shame is a burden to them. When you reduce shame, you are leaving room for the development of guilt. The question is how you might do that.

If you are troubled by shame, there is a good chance it developed in childhood during the process of socialization when your parents conveyed to you the difference between right and wrong.

Shame is likely to have become excessive during this process if any of the following took place:

- Discipline was harsh and excessive.
- Discipline involved isolation and perceived rejection.
- Your parents did not repair the relationship between them and you following discipline.
- Your parents routinely criticized your thoughts, feelings, and wishes, rather than restricting their evaluations to your behaviors.
- You experienced trauma that you believed was your fault.

Your greatest means for reducing shame is to reflect on it. Here are some questions to consider:

Did the mistakes you made or the discipline you received in childhood occur because you were a bad or unlovable person?
Do you have to be perfect?
Why should you be ashamed of your thoughts, feelings, and wishes?
Are mistakes able to serve as an opportunity to learn or are they a sign of your being a failure?
Are you a good person and are you doing the best you can?

Reflecting on shame allows you to reduce its grip on your mind, on your thoughts, through which you created excuses, blamed your friend, minimized the problem, deceived yourself, or became angry at yourself or your friend when there was difficulty between you. It is liberating to know that you are able to make a mistake, learn from it, acknowledge it to your friend, and improve your relationship. Now, with realistic guilt following a mistake, you are able to address it and repair the relationship.

Reflecting on shame and reducing it will be easier when your friend or partner addresses any of your behaviors that are difficult for him or her, without shaming you. You are accepted for who you are, while your behavior may be criticized. Shame is also likely to be less when you know that your relationship is strong enough to withstand conflicts. You are able to address them safely.

Also, speaking about your shame to your partner when your partner simply listens with empathy as you relate your sense of being bad and worthless will greatly help you in reducing your shame. Ask your partner not to reassure you that you are a good person because when you are in a state of shame you are not likely to believe such comments, you will resist your partner's experience of you, and you might even do something worse to prove yourself right. It is better if your partner simply acknowledges your shame with empathy, saying, for example, "It must be so hard to think that you're worthless whenever you make a mistake. You're really hard on yourself. I'm sorry you're so convinced that you're worthless. You're in so much pain now. Tell me and I'll listen." When someone responds with empathy to your expressions of shame you will begin to doubt your shame-based self-perceptions and be open to the possibility that you have more worth than you generally experience about yourself.

Exercise

Reflect on an event that you experienced shame about. Writing your reactions to the items in this exercise may be helpful.

1. Describe the feeling of shame and its associated thoughts and bodily sensations.
2. Reflect on possible triggers in that event that activated the shame.
3. Be as specific as possible about what you did, or what another person said about you or about what you did, that is associated with the shame.
4. Reflect on possible causes of your behavior that are not related to shame.
5. Differentiate your behavior from your sense of self.
6. If your behavior affected another person, acknowledge it to the other person with the goal of repairing the relationship.

Loss

As you get to know someone and enjoy your time with that person, he or she becomes a part of your life, associated with your favored activities and interests, and eventually a part of how you define yourself: "I'm Sue's partner"; "I'm John's best friend." If the other person is an attachment figure, you begin to turn to him or her for comfort and support, relying on the person to assist you in managing stressful situations and in making difficult decisions. You begin to share aspects of yourself that are private, not revealed to acquaintances and casual friends. You show yourself as more vulnerable and especially more vulnerable to the loss of this relationship. If your friend seems to be withdrawing from the relationship, or if he or she actually ends it, you are at risk of feeling rejected or abandoned. When someone has had an increasingly important place in your mind and heart, you are left with a sense of emptiness, grief, and possibly despair if the person dies or chooses to leave the relationship. The deep sense of meaning and joy that comes from a healthy relationship necessarily also brings deep sadness and grief at the loss of that relationship.

You may find that accepting the reality of loss is harder than reading about it. If loss was a strong factor in your attachment history, through death, divorce, or other kinds of separations, you may have a hard time embracing love because you are so aware of the pain of loss. You may also have difficulty trusting that your relationships will last long enough to make them worthwhile when the inevitable loss comes. Reflecting on your past losses may well help. If your father seldom spent time with you, you may have originally concluded that you were lacking in what your father would have loved, that it was your fault for being unlovable. Through the gift of reflection you may well realize that your father was challenged in his relationship with your mother, with other relatives and friends, and with all his children. You may have experienced deep shame in relation to your father and you may slide into shame in the face of minor conflicts with, differences with, and separations from friends. Reflecting on this process and recognizing emerging feelings of shame may help you to inhibit those feelings and be open to the positive features of your friends' interactions with you.

Anticipating that your relationship could end and being vulnerable to its loss may well have you on the verge of negative emotions such as anxiety, sadness, and anger. If you obsess about the possibility of loss or if you dwell on possible events that could end the relationship, you will not truly enjoy and be satisfied with the relationship. Being habitually insecure about the strength of the relationship is likely to reduce its strength. If the fear of the pain of loss is too great, you might even avoid meaningful relationships. You may assume that relationships don't last and that the short-term pleasure of having a relationship is outweighed by the inevitable, much larger pain of the relationship ending. In the example involving Ann Marie and Brenda, above, Ann Marie's fear of the loss of the relationship would no doubt have made the relationship less satisfying for Brenda, which would then make the relationship more likely to end. If Ann Marie were able to reflect on her fears, talk with Brenda about her perceptions, and trust Brenda's response, the relationship would be more stable.

Denying that loss is painful is not a useful approach; nor is dwelling on the pain of loss. Attachment relationships provide deep satisfaction and joy in life while their loss is the source of much of life's pain. Clinging to relationships in the denial of the possibility of loss and avoiding all relationships in order to avoid the reality of loss are both unsatisfying strategies. The former reminds us of the preoccupied attachment classification mentioned earlier while the latter is similar to the dismissive attachment classification.

The middle way—similar to the path of Buddhism—is acceptance. Acceptance of the deep meaning and joy offered by healthy relationships. And acceptance of the fact that nothing is permanent. And acceptance of the pain when the relationship ends—as it is certain to do by death, if not before. *Love* and *loss* go together.

Yes, when you seek and attain love, when you value it and organize your life around it, you place yourself at the edge of great pain, knowing that your relationship with your partner will end, if only in death. Just as you need to accept death to truly value life, you need to accept the loss of love to truly value love. Deeply loving your partner brings acceptance of the possibility of losing your partner and living each day with your partner as if it were your last. (Certainly this is considered to be a cliché. Certainly it is very true nevertheless).

The Developing Relationship

As you and another person get to know each other, you each discover whether you are compatible in ways that are important to you. If you are, you continue the relationship; if not, you go your separate ways. As you begin a relationship, the early weeks and months bring uncertainties, misunderstandings, and differences. And that's only the beginning!

As your relationship with someone develops further—as the person becomes more and more important to you—so too can the emotions of anxiety. You are likely to be more sensitive to perceived rejections, signs of indifference, or expressions of conflict. You may be more vulnerable now—the pain will be greater if the relationship ends than it would have been at the onset. As your emotions become more intense your ability to regulate them becomes more necessary.

When another person is becoming important to you, you may be close to feeling insecure until you feel certain that the relationship is for better or for worse. Casual friendships do not provoke this sense of insecurity because if they end for whatever reason, the relationship was never important enough to fret over. Yes, in the development of a relationship that is becoming important there is likely to be an edge to it that generates some anxiety. How intense the anxiety is and how you manage it depends on many factors from your past and present. But anxiety will probably be there, whether in the background or in the foreground of your life. If Ann Marie, again from the example above, were able to confidently believe that her relationship with Brenda had developed so that it was for better or for worse, she probably would not have gone through the strong negative emotions in response to the routine stresses common to any relationship. Until commitment emerges in the relationship, whereby the two individuals believe that the relationship is more important than the instances of conflict, anxiety is likely to be present if the relationship has moved beyond a casual acquaintance.

Conflicting Emotions

As a relationship becomes more and more important to you, it is certainly going to become associated with more varied, complex, and intense emotions. On a typical week when you are developing a relationship with a possible partner, you are likely to feel excitement, hope, passion, pleasure, pleasant anticipation, and affection. At the same time you may feel anxiety, sadness, frustration, anger, shame, and guilt because of the developing place that your friend has in your life. So why do those negative emotions arise along with the positive ones? There are several reasons for this circumstance:

The Experience of Being Evaluated

As the relationship is developing and there is no commitment to it yet, you cannot escape the reality that you are being evaluated, just as you are evaluating the other person. As we discussed earlier, when you are evaluated, you tend to become somewhat defensive, to be aware of the need to protect yourself. This is bound to keep you mildly to moderately tense when thinking of or interacting in your relationship: "What does she think about what I did? What is the best way to please her? That was a mistake! She's disappointed in me." Such thoughts make it difficult to relax in the relationship, feel accepted, and remain open and engaged with the other.

Self-Doubts about Relationship Skills

With the backdrop of evaluation, you are at risk of analyzing your functioning in the relationship and noticing any of your behaviors that might possibly be taken the wrong way, be a sign of selfishness or insensitivity, or demonstrate some deficiency in relationship skills.

Perceptions of Negative Motives in the Partner's Behavior

As the relationship becomes more important, you are more likely to become vigilant about the meaning of the other person's behavior. Your fear of loss may give a negative perceptual set so that if the other person does withdraw from the relationship, it might not hurt so much. Being insecure in the relationship might well undermine the relationship through possible conflicts that emerge when you assume negative motives for the behaviors of the other. When Ann Marie was bothered because Brenda was in a bad mood, her distress probably involved her assumption that Brenda was annoyed with her.

Misunderstandings and Differences of Opinion

As you are getting to know another person, relating at a level deeper than that of a casual friend, there are certain to be misunderstandings and differences. These may place some stress on the relationship, especially if they are not acknowledged by you or the other. If they are addressed, they can be accepted and, ideally, resolved. Differences of opinion need to be understood in order to know whether they are a threat to the relationship. Conflicts, too, need to be understood and addressed. The ability to repair relationships (covered in Key 7) is crucial if the relationship is to remain secure. However, such efforts at repair are often themselves associated with anxiety and possibly anger, shame, or guilt.

Transition from Idealism to Realism

In the early stages of getting to know another person, we tend to look at things through rose-colored glasses. The other's positive traits seem magnificent and all pervasive, while any negative traits are minimized, if they are seen at all. As reality sets in, doubts appear, felt by you and the other person. You and your partner need to face reality, and in doing so, you know that the relationship is now more insecure while you both determine if these emerging, less appealing qualities of each other are deal breakers or not.

Reduction in Independence
A relationship adds a great deal to your life, and so you work to deepen it and ensure its continuity. However, the relationship also brings some restrictions to your independence, along with responsibilities you did not have previously. Integrating the wishes, interests, and plans of the other person into your life will necessarily involve some negotiations and compromises that require you to give up some things that you might prefer doing. How willing you are to compromise and the degree of importance you place on things you might have to give up or cut back on will influence whether what you receive from a relationship outweighs what you have to give up in order to have it.

Anger

Anger is another emotion that may, though not always, arise when you're in a developing relationship. You may be a mild-mannered person in much of your life and then frequently find yourself in a state of anger when you are in an important relationship. As you begin to care more for another person, you find yourself being angry with that person more often. What is that about? Some answers follow.

Need for Control in Your Relationship
More than likely your anger reflects your vulnerable emotions of anxiety, self-doubt, and shame. If you feel insecure about your relationship you are likely to anticipate its loss and therefore feel vulnerable. If this feeling becomes habitual and intense most likely you will find yourself trying to control the behavior of your

friend or partner. Your security seems to become connected to your partner doing what you want him or her to be doing. As long as he or she acts a certain way, you can experience some confidence that this person cares for you and is committed to the relationship. When he or she does not act that way, you experience the person as uncaring, insensitive, or selfish. You must not be important to him or her after all. You become angry as you experience the person as violating an unspoken agreement that he or she will act in ways that you consider to demonstrate his care and commitment.

Children who are extremely insecure in their relationships with their caregivers tend to be very controlling. They want things to be their way and when they are not, they often become angry. Their anger is their way of managing their anxiety about not being important enough to their parents to feel safe that they will be cared for. If you find yourself frequently becoming angry with your partner for doing things that you wish that he or she did not do, more than likely you are feeling a similar degree of anxiety to the insecure child. Your attachment relationship is threatened.

Domestic violence—the most severe form of anger within important relationships—tends to be grounded in the fear of loss, of being rejected, that the person is not able to reflect on, talk about, and resolve. The insecurity that the person feels may be habitual and intense and based on the meaning he gives to his partner's behavior that has nothing to do with the meaning that his partner gives to that behavior. His partner may have failed to pick up something for him at the store that he had asked for and he interprets this act of forgetfulness as representing his partner's no longer caring for him or even as being caused by his partner's having been out with someone else. All from forgetting to bring home a snack! When such insecurity and subsequent anger is that intense, most often the person is struggling with shame. No matter what his partner says or does, he always has doubts that he is lovable to his partner. Doubting himself that he is worthy of love, he does not trust that the love is genuine and lasting, no matter what his partner does to reassure him.

Domestic violence is an extreme form of anger and control; it shows the connection between the two as well as the sense of vulnerability that underlies this desire to control your partner and your anger when you cannot do so. Efforts to manage your anger are likely to be much more successful if you are able to reflect on and communicate with your partner about your anxieties about the relationship. If you are unable to see how the roots of your anger often extend into your vulnerabilities about your relationship, then you will likely find reasons in your partner and your partner's behavior to justify your anger. That leaves you with the belief that your partner is responsible for your "anger problem." If he only acted in a certain way you would not become angry!

Better to do the following:

- Identify the likely insecurities that might underlie your anger.
- Acknowledge them to yourself and reflect on their possible roots in past attachment relationships and related emotions of loss, shame, and loneliness.
- Discuss them with your partner to explore qualities of your current relationship that might contribute to your insecurity and doubts and seek a resolution.

If you need to acknowledge that you tend to be a "controlling" person, you might give thought to the possibility that this is not a personality trait as much as a way of coping with insecurity in your relationships.

Difficulty Addressing Conflicts and Differences
You might be so gentle and mild mannered that your periodic intense angry outbursts toward your partner confuse or even frighten you. This might suggest that you have difficulty dealing with conflicts and differences and tend to avoid them, not think about them, and hope that they will simply go away. Or you leave subtle hints or suggestions that something is bothering you without being clear about what it is and how much it bothers you. In this case the fact

that you are bothered by your partner's behavior does not suggest that you have a need to control your partner. It may mean that you are not comfortable telling him or her that you are bothered.

Being able to communicate clearly when something in your partner's behavior is bothering you is often described as being assertive. Assertiveness—giving expression to your wishes, thoughts, preferences, and perceptions—simply reflects your belief that you are an equal partner in the relationship. There is no need for you to defer to your partner's wishes. If the two of you differ, then your assertiveness reflects your belief that these differences exist and should be discussed in a manner that is open and balanced. Your wishes are given neither more nor less value than your partner's wishes. Assertiveness—being comfortable with differences with your partner and naming those differences clearly and openly— goes a long way toward integrating conflicts and differences that exist in all relationships. To be effective, both partners need to be comfortable with being assertive.

If you have difficulty being assertive, your first effort to have a place for your preferences in your relationship might well be to send subtle signals about what you want and hope that your partner will act on them. If he does not, you might look for other ways to attain your goals, without his having to actively change his preferences. If that fails, you may be at risk of withdrawing into passivity and being resigned that your preferences will not have a place in the relationship. Or you may explode in anger over your partner's selfish behavior.

Finally, it should be noted that troubles with anger in your relationship may relate to expectations of differences for men and women in relationships. Historically, in many societies, the preferences of the man are given priority over the preferences of the woman. She should defer to his wishes without acknowledging her own. Or if she gives voice to her wishes, she should accept his decision on whose preferences are given priority.

In considering the two aspects of anger just discussed—insecurity about your relationship and difficulty addressing conflicts and differences—you might give thought to whether these factors related more to gender differences than to factors unique to you and your partner. If you are a man and you find yourself wanting to control your partner and become angry when she does not do what you want, this may reflect an assumption that your wishes should take priority over hers and that she wants it her way too much, when in fact she may want an open and balanced exploration of both of your wishes. If you are a woman and tend to have difficulty speaking assertively about your preferences, this might reflect an assumption that your wishes should have a lower priority than those of your partner. If one or both of these possibilities are present in your relationship, you are likely to have greater difficulty dealing with differences without resorting to anger.

Exercise
Reflect on an event in a relationship that made you angry.

1. Describe the feeling of anger and associated thoughts and bodily sensations.
2. Be as specific as possible about what the other person did that preceded your anger.
3. What assumptions did you have about why the person acted that way?
4. Consider other possibilities for his or her behavior.
5. Consider other emotions that might have been under your anger (sadness, anxiety, shame, loss).
6. Consider how you might have expressed your anger differently in order to better address the situation and repair the relationship (if desirable).

Characteristics of Emotional Competence

So far in this chapter I've outlined several positive and negative emotions that are common to relationships and how to respond to them. To make sense of it all, here are three important features of emotional competence to bear in mind.

Knowing What You Feel

This may be more difficult than you think. Over the years you may have developed the habit of not noticing your feelings, for many reasons. As a child your parents may have communicated that certain feelings were not acceptable. Anger may have been something that was selfish. Fears may have been seen as immature. Doubts may have been a sign that you were insecure. Sadness may have signified weakness. Pride may have always been a sign of being conceited. Joy may have been naïveté. Love may have been dependency. And there may have been many variations on the above.

If feelings were judged as being right or wrong during your childhood, you may judge your feelings to be right or wrong now. You might then have the habit of not noticing your "wrong" feelings. You may talk yourself out of them. You may feel shame over having a certain feeling and then avoid thinking about it and never learn what it means in your life. If you habitually judge your feelings, there is a strong likelihood that you often do not know what you are feeling. Even if you do know what the feeling is, you are not likely to know why it is there and what it means. Feelings represent aspects of your experiences with the people, events, and objects of your life. They are signals of or clues to the meanings of these aspects of your life. Judging them often interferes with what they are trying to tell you about your partner, an event, or an object.

For emotional competence it is wise to develop the habit of accepting whatever feeling you have without evaluating it. Accepting it does not mean that you have to act on it. Rather, you note it, wonder where it came from and what it means, and ask yourself whether it is suggesting that you continue on with or change your planned course of action.

If you have a vague feeling of being relaxed or being ill at ease, you might be wise to remain aware of the feeling, allowing your mind to wander, to see what might be associated with either one of those feelings. Further reflection might make it more clear why you are feeling positive or negative, with this new clarity leading you to a course of action that is in your best interest. These vague feelings are sometimes called "gut feelings" and may well be a better guide for what is best for you than trying to take a rational approach that considers various facts to determine which choice is the best.

Communicating Your Feelings

When you communicate your feelings to your partner in an open and clear manner, you are necessarily integrating your emotions with your reflective ability in order to make them understandable to your partner. Since communicating your feelings is easier said than done, the next chapter is devoted to *mastering communication*. Your feelings will also meet with your partner's understanding and perspective, which will prevent them from being influenced by assumptions, fears, and doubts that might have originated in your past.

In communicating your feelings, it is wise to own them. Rather than saying, "You made me angry," it would be better to say, "I am angry that you . . ."

Better too is being receptive to changing your feelings following a response from your partner: "Now that I understand better I can see that my anger was premature."

Even better is to inhibit the development of a feeling before you know your partner's perspective: "Thanks for helping me to understand. I couldn't figure out why you did that (and since I could not figure it out I did not get prematurely angry)."

Also, it is wise to think about your intention in communicating your feelings. Is it to prove yourself right and your partner wrong? Is it to hurt your partner if you feel that your partner hurt you? Is it to share your experience of your partner and his or her behavior clearly so that he or she has an opportunity to respond? Is it to repair your relationship if you are experiencing a problem with it? Is it to become closer to your partner when you are experiencing positive feelings about him or her and your relationship? The effects on your relationship of communicating your feelings about it are often determined by your intention in communicating in the first place.

Managing Your Feelings

The integration of your reflective competence with your emotional life is the most effective way by far to manage your feelings. When you have a clear awareness of your inner life and a realistic understanding of the inner life of your partner, your feelings are likely to be grounded in the present circumstances and less influenced by assumptions, doubts, and memories from the past. Your reflective functioning gives words to your inner life that enable you to identify and communicate your feelings clearly. This integration of your reflective and emotional lives enables you to maintain perspective on what's happening by recalling your histories together as well as the goals and dreams that you and your partner both have about the future. Reflecting on your emotional response to a situation prevents you from experiencing the current situation in all-or-nothing extremes and enables you to inhibit an emotional reaction to an event and instead develop an emotional response that considers the big picture.

Exercises

1. Are you comfortable with positive emotions? Sometimes, because of our past experiences of shame and loss, we are not able to accept and enjoy positive emotions. If you have difficulty with positive emotions, you might reflect on the following:

   - Are you comfortable with both loving someone *and* being loved by that person or do you prefer relationships characterized by one or the other but not both?
   - Are you comfortable feeling gratitude for something your partner has done for you or does that make you feel too vulnerable?

- Are you comfortable feeling pleasure and passion or do those feelings elicit guilt or shame?
- Are you comfortable with excitement or does it make you anxious?

2. Are you comfortable with negative emotions?

   - Does fear become terror?
   - Does sadness lead to despair?
   - Does anger create rage?
   - Do negative feelings lead you to see yourself as being *bad* or *selfish*?

MASTER EFFECTIVE COMMUNICATION

Why is it so hard to talk to people with whom we have important relationships? We know our friend or partner well; we have much in common and we have similar goals. Given those strengths in the relationship, shouldn't we be able to use them as a foundation to easily explore our thoughts and feelings, our differences and dreams? Sometimes we don't reflect enough on what we think and what our partner thinks. Sometimes our emotions become intense and take priority over our reflecting. Sometimes we avoid certain topics. Even in close relationships, sometimes the range of topics that are not discussed would fill a notebook. And sometimes we simply do not give enough thought to our communications and how crucial they are to developing, deepening, and maintaining our important relationships.

Let's explore the nature and value of effective communication, its challenges, and how to improve it.

Taking Turns

All effective communication is reciprocal. When one person talks, the other person listens and then responds to what the first person said. The first person listens to the second person's response and then responds to what he or she said. This talk-listen-talk or listen-talk-listen is now complete unless the second person needs more clarity, wants to introduce another, related theme, or wants to express disagreement. Communication needs to be complete if it is to be effective. If either person begins another topic before the first topic has been completed, both are left with uncertainty about what has been understood or agreed to.

This reciprocal pattern of communication is also primary in the interpersonal dialogue that occurs between a parent and infant. And they do it without the child's contributing any words. In a period of 15/100 of a second after the infant initiates an expression, the parent tends to respond with a similar expression, and 15/100 of a second later the infant replies. They are sharing experiences, and when the parent matches the affective expression of the infant with a similar expression, the infant knows that the parent understands him or her and is responding. The parent's response is contingent on the infant's expression, rather than being a random act separate from the child. Dan Stern, an influential theorist and researcher on the interpersonal development of infants, who studied this pattern years ago, says that this matching occurs according to intensity, rhythm, beat, contour, shape, and duration. Matching occurs with facial expressions, voice modulations and rhythms, gestures, posture, and timing. This communication is nonverbal, yet the infant and parent both know that they are engaged, they are important to each other, they notice each other, and they are sharing delight and enjoyment around a given experience—whether the experience is their delight in each other or in their excitement about a particularly colorful and musical toy.

Children who have been exposed to neglect or maltreatment, whether it be physical, sexual, emotional, or verbal, often are not good at such reciprocal dialogues with adults. They often do not participate in these preverbal dialogues of interest and delight, nor, when they are older, do they participate well in verbal communications. Many say little, just listening to the adult who is talking to them. Others talk constantly but have trouble listening to an adult's response. Others do not maintain focus, talking about many seemingly unrelated things or distracting the adult from what he or she is intent on discussing. Other children have reasonably coherent communications around light themes but have great difficulty communicating about stressful events or things that they have done wrong.

Many children who were not maltreated still do not have habits of effective communication if these habits were not encouraged in their developing years. "Children should be seen and not heard" is an adage that has been long out of fashion. Nevertheless, many open, direct, clear, and honest communications from children to their parents are viewed as disrespectful. We might tell our children that they may tell us if they are angry with something we did, but if they raise their voice and show anger in their facial expressions, they are in trouble. Yet to say that you are angry in a quiet, friendly, relaxed voice is ambiguous and confusing. It might be taken as dishonest, since anger is not expressed that way. It could be extremely confusing for your children to be told that when they express anger toward you it's called disrespect, but when you express anger toward them, it's called discipline and it is they who are responsible for your anger. There is often very little in the way of equality when it has to do with the expression of anger in parent-child relationships.

Another type of difficulty is that some adults have trouble alternating between talking and listening in their communications with others. Some are unusually quiet and noncommunicative, while others engage in monologues, giving no sign of being interested in what the other person is saying.

Reciprocal communication requires the open and engaged state of mind that was discussed earlier. If you're defensive, you're primarily focused on protecting your perspective and plan of action and are not open to being influenced by the viewpoints of the other person. When you're open and engaged, your mind goes quickly back and forth between a focus on your inner life while you're addressing the other and a focus on the other's inner life as you attend to his or her communication to you. This is a rapid process, since while you're communicating you're also aware of the effect of your communication on the other person, which you gauge by noting his or her nonverbal expressions. In fact the nonverbal expressions of the other person have an impact on what you are aware of in your inner life, influencing the memories about which you are reflecting. The better you know each other, the more likely you are to have mutual influence in this fluid, synchronized fashion.

Example

Ben and Cathy had spoken about going to a movie in the evening. They discussed their plan that afternoon:

BEN: I didn't see any movies I thought that we'd like so I made reservations at the Steak House instead.

CATHY: I really was hoping to just see a movie. How about sitting down with me and looking through the options again?

BEN: That would be a waste of time. I know there's nothing showing that I want to see.

CATHY: Let's look over what's playing together before deciding.

BEN: I already made reservations for the restaurant.

CATHY: And if we do go out to eat, I'd rather not go to the Steak House again.

BEN: Fine! You decide then, and let me know what you come up with.

In this example the only value Ben saw in communicating with Cathy was to tell her what he had decided. When she communicated that she wanted to decide together how to spend the evening, he became defensive.

How much better would it have been if the conversation went something like this:

BEN: I know we talked about seeing a movie tonight but I couldn't find anything that I thought would be good. Do you have a minute so we could look at what's playing together and see if we come up with anything? If not, we might just go out to eat.

CATHY: I have a minute now. *(They look over the description of the eight movies showing at the local cinema.)* I agree, nothing there that I'd like to see either. Any thoughts about where you'd like to eat?

BEN: I'm in the mood for the Steak House.

CATHY: And I'm a little tired of going there so often. How about sushi?

BEN: Italian?

CATHY: Italian is fine. But not the one on Third Street.

BEN: OK. I heard there's a new place down on State Street. Should I try to get reservations there?

CATHY: Sounds good to me.

In this second scenario Ben left room for Cathy to contribute to the decision. Sometimes there's simply a lack of taking turns in discussing an event.

Here, Jake wants to talk about a change at work, but he does not want to hear Abe's thoughts.

JAKE: I don't think John is being at all fair in deciding that there'll be a new formula in working out our commission.

ABE: He did seek our input and . . .

JAKE: It's going to make it a lot harder to get a bonus when we make a sale.

ABE: John mentioned that and pointed out . . .

JAKE: He always has an excuse — he calls it a reason — for what he does that makes his life easier.

ABE: I thought he went overboard to make it fair by . . .

JAKE: I'd like to see what he'd do if we just worked less.

ABE: My guess is that he'd try to know . . .

JAKE: Why are you always taking his side? Have you worked out a separate deal with him?

In such "communication" there is little that is reciprocal. Here Jake simply wants Abe to listen to him and agree with his views.

Jake has no interest in Abe's views and is certainly not open to leaving room for them to influence his own. If this occurs in one discussion, there is a good chance it will occur in others as well—and an equally good chance that Abe will withdraw from the friendship.

A reciprocal communication would have looked like this:

JAKE: I don't think John is being at all fair in deciding there'll be a new formula in working out our commission.

ABE: He did seek our input and detailed the pros and cons of the change for us. Did you give him the feedback he asked for?

JAKE: I didn't bother. I figured it was a waste of time . . . that he'd already made up his mind.

ABE: Actually he asked me to talk with him about one of my concerns. He made a few changes and then I was fine with that section of the plan.

JAKE: He really listened and made some changes?

ABE: I think so. I'm comfortable giving the new formula a chance. He said we'd review it in two months.

JAKE: I guess I didn't think about it much. I'm probably too sensitive to the boss making decisions that affect me so I don't even pay attention to what he's deciding and if he wants our input. Thanks, Abe.

Saying Everything You Mean

For your communication with your friend or partner to be effective, you'll need to be clear and complete in what you say. Often miscommunications occur when you give your friend a bit of what you want her to know and assume she knows the rest. Because of your history together you make assumptions about her understanding what you mean. However, she thinks you meant something different and acts on her own assumption. It is better to take an extra few minutes and be redundant rather than act on faulty assumptions.

Example

Jane sometimes stopped at a pub after work with Tiffany and Rita, two friends she had come to know through their work together on a particular project. She had more in common with Tiffany than with Rita but enjoyed the company of both. One day she was troubled about a medical worry that she had, one that she knew Tiffany's sister had dealt with in the past. She urgently wanted some advice and information, but she did not want the office to know about it. At work she asked Tiffany if she had time to stop at the pub after work that day. Tiffany responded that she would be glad to; later, when she saw Rita, she invited her along. Jane was intensely disappointed when she saw that Rita was with Tiffany at the pub. She wanted to talk about her worry but did not want Rita to know. She did not say anything and later left feeling dissatisfied. Tiffany and Rita were puzzled and disappointed that Jane was withdrawn but would not tell them what was bothering her.

This problem could have been avoided if Jane had told Tiffany there was something on her mind that she wanted to talk about with her, alone. Jane had assumed that since she did not mention Rita, Tiffany would not ask her along without first asking Jane. Tiffany simply assumed that since the three of them had always gone out together, Jane had just forgotten to mention Rita or that Jane would normally have assumed that Tiffany would invite Rita along. The mistake could have easily been avoided if Jane had told Tiffany that there was something on her mind that she wanted to discuss with her privately or if Tiffany had asked if Jane wanted Tiffany to invite Rita.

The more we know our friend or partner, the more we begin to make assumptions about what he or she thinks, feels, wants, or would say about something. As our assumptions increase, our chances of miscommunicating or not communicating at all about important matters also increase. Sometimes we communicate verbally but, by ignoring the nonverbal, fail to have complete communication.

You might tell your partner that you like the idea of the art festival that will be in town next weekend. However, you mention it in passing, much as you might comment that you saw an interesting bird or liked a certain kind of coffee. Your partner notes that you have a positive opinion of the art festival and fails to connect it with how much you want to go because of the casual way that you mentioned it. He or she would have been much more likely to know that you wanted to go to the festival if you had said with animation and excitement, "I read about the art festival coming next weekend and it really looks great! There are two or three new parts this year and I'd like to see them. It could be the best festival we've had in years."

The animation and detail would have clearly conveyed how much you wanted to go to the festival. If there was any doubt, you might have added: "I checked and it's going to be sunny Saturday but might rain Sunday. I'd love to go Saturday. Would you like to go too?"

Asking for What You Want

Another ingredient of effective communication is clarity and completeness in asking your friend or partner for what you want. Too often you may assume that your friend knows what you want, so you don't need to ask for it. If your friend does not know what you want and you think he or she should know, you are likely to become angry about your friend's failure to anticipate the wishes that you had left unspoken.

When you have a long history with your friend that includes doing many similar things in similar situations, it is reasonable to assume that your friend is likely to remember that something is important to you. When he or she does something for you, says something to you, or gives you what you want without your asking, your assumption gets stronger and you anticipate that he or she will always think of your wishes. One day, however, your friend is preoccupied and forgets to do what you have come to expect him or her to do. Then you may well become annoyed, thinking that he or she was selfish or in his or her own little world. You may think you would never have forgotten something that was important to your friend. You may go further and think that maybe your relationship is not as important as it once was to your friend, certainly not as important as the relationship is to you. So you withdraw a bit, assuming that this will convey your being hurt or annoyed at your friend's forgetting your wish and that he or she will apologize and make it right. However, your friend either does not notice that you are not as engaged with him or her as you usually are or your friend does not think that it has anything to do with his or her behavior. By withdrawing, you were reminding your friend of his or her forgetfulness, and it went unnoticed! Essentially you did not clearly ask for what you wanted again—that your friend remember that he or she forgot—just as you did not ask for what you wanted the first time.

Example

Kate and Jennifer had been partners for several months. Kate loved going out on weekends, while Jennifer was content staying home. Usually Kate would suggest that they go somewhere on Saturday or Sunday and almost always Jennifer agreed to go too. Kate was aware that she was the one who always asked, so she decided not to do so and instead waited for Jennifer to suggest going out. She waited over the next three weekends, but Jennifer never asked. Kate grew increasingly annoyed because she thought that Jennifer certainly knew that Kate wanted to go out on the weekends, so she should have suggested it herself rather than waiting for Kate to always have to bring it up. Kate felt that she was begging to always be the one to ask, but now she felt annoyed that Jennifer did not offer to go out, knowing how important it was to Kate. Kate showed her annoyance over another weekend and Jennifer actually did not know what Kate was annoyed about! When Kate told her, she ended by saying, "But you should have known!"

Kate could have prevented the problem if she had simply kept going out and asking Jennifer if she wanted to go too. If she felt it was too one sided, that she was begging Jennifer to go along with something she wanted to do, then she should have clearly communicated that to Jennifer. The conversation could have gone something like this:

KATE: Jennifer, I know you seldom seem to suggest that we go out on the weekends. Almost always I'm the one who does the asking. I'm beginning to feel that maybe you're just doing me a favor in going out with me — that you'd rather not go but you do it out of obligation. Do you feel trapped about going out because I ask? Would you rather stay home?

JENNIFER: Thanks for asking, but I'm fine about your always taking the initiative. You're right that I'm often more comfortable just hanging out at home than you are. But I know that going out is important to you so I'm happy to go out with you. If I really want to stay home all weekend sometime, I'll let you know.

When either you or your partner takes most of the initiative for what you do in your relationship, there is a danger that the relationship will become one sided. It becomes the responsibility of the one who takes the initiative to provide interests for both. Often the person who does not take the initiative says, "I don't really care what we do; I'd enjoy doing whatever you'd like to do." On the surface that seems altruistic — doing what your partner wants — but in practice it may become a burden to your partner to always have to come up with something for both of you to do. Plus, a relationship thrives when both people contribute to it — interests, ideas, passions, and energy. Make a place for your agenda too — you might be surprised to find that your partner will be grateful.

For good communication in a healthy relationship it is important to remember the following:

- Asking for what you want is not selfish.

- Your partner is not selfish when he or she doesn't know what you did not ask for.
- Not asking for what you want places all the responsibility on your partner to take the initiative.
- Asking for what you want allows you to contribute your share to the relationship.

Matching Nonverbal Expressions to Your Words

As has been mentioned a number of times so far, if communication is to be effective, it needs to be clear. Ambiguity certainly increases the risk of miscommunication and unnecessary arguments. One of the best ways to enhance clarity is to have congruence between your verbal and nonverbal communications.

You are likely to forget nonverbal communication when you speak of the need for more effective communication. Yet research has found that most of our social and emotional communications are nonverbal rather than verbal. If that is true, it is certainly important that you both use your nonverbal means of communicating and also that your nonverbal communications are congruent with your verbal statements.

As soon as you begin communicating through text, email, and voice mail, you begin to bring more ambiguity into your communications, thus increasing the danger of misunderstandings. The reason for this is much more than the brevity of the communication. More important is the lack of explicit nonverbal communications along with the verbal statements. Face-to-face communications are much more effective for clear communications as long as you take advantage of the power of nonverbal expressions in a clear and congruent manner.

The following three examples are of nonverbal communication that is not helpful for attaining the healthy relationships that this book hopes to assist.

1. You may have difficulty expressing anger toward a friend or partner and as a result, you may smile or speak quietly while tell-

ing someone you are angry with him. This may lead him to un-derestimate how strongly you feel about something that he did, and he may not take it as seriously as you had intended. Better to express your anger through words and the facial expressions and tone of voice that convey anger across a wide range of cultures. While some believe that angry facial expressions are disrespectful, rude, or aggressive, in my experience these characteristics can be attributed to the words themselves.

2. You may be anxious about an upcoming event but in describ-ing it to a friend you speak with composure and joke around a bit, trying to make light of your feelings. Your friend does not know that you are experiencing dread and does not offer to go with you to the event or show other signs of support. You are disappointed in your friend for her seeming indifference to your distress, which you had minimized nonverbally. You were left to handle the situa-tion alone—increasing your anxiety—since she did not know that you wanted help.

3. You completed a project that was very important to you and you anxiously awaited the results. You casually told your partner about it when he asked why you seemed preoccupied. When your project was accepted, you spoke about it in a matter-of-fact way, not wanting to seem like you were bragging, while in fact you were ecstatic. Later you were disappointed that no one seemed to be happy over your success. But in fact your partner's reaction matched his perception of your own, which was an understate-ment of what you really felt.

In these three examples the ambiguity of the communications, resulting from a lack of—or incongruent—nonverbal expression, created miscommunication about how important something was to you. When there is congruence between the nonverbal and verbal, the communication is much more clear. When there is a lack of congruence, we tend to trust the nonverbal expression more than the verbal when assessing the meaning of the commu-nication. Saying that something is important to us, with a voice that is matter-of-fact and with composed facial expressions, is like-ly to create a lack of awareness in our friend or partner about how important it actually is to us. Saying that you are not bothered by something while your face and voice display anger is likely to convince your friend that you are angry and that you have a reason for hiding it.

Why don't we more clearly express our experience of an event nonverbally? Several reasons can be suggested:

- You are more exposed because your nonverbal expressions may reveal very clearly what you are thinking and feeling.
- Being exposed, you are vulnerable if your excitement is not shared or leads to disappointment. If you show pride, others may view you as conceited.
- You're vulnerable if you're sad or frightened and others either don't seem to care or make fun of you for being weak.
- You're vulnerable if you're angry and others think you're selfish.
- You may have been raised to understate your reactions, to be modest.
- You may prefer to conceal your emotions, and since nonverbal communication reveals emotion much more than verbal statements, you refrain from nonverbal expression.

While the motivations behind these reasons may be justified in contexts in which you relate with strangers or acquaintances, they are likely to compromise your deeper relationships. Healthy relationships involve sharing your important thoughts, feelings, and wishes, trusting that your partner is interested in them, accepts them, and will join you in the way that is best for you. When you support your words with nonverbal expressions that match your inner life, you will be better understood and experience greater emotional intimacy.

Exercise

This exercise is beneficial for your exploration of the importance of nonverbal communication.

1. Find two friends to engage in this exercise with you.
2. Think of an interesting or humorous story to tell your friend that will take about 4 minutes to tell.
3. Start telling your story to your friend, who is instructed to listen attentively.
4. After 1 minute 15 seconds have a third person say, "Stop listening," at which point your friend looks at the floor and gives no nonverbal responses to your story.
5. After another 1 minute 15 seconds have the third person say, "Listen again," at which point your friend looks at you and responds to your story nonverbally until you come to the end of the story.
6. Tell your friend your experience of telling your story when he or she was not listening. Reflect on how it affected your thinking, emotions, motivation, and anything else that you noticed as well as the story itself.
7. Have your friend tell a story as you listen; repeat the preceding steps.

Separating Facts from Experience

There are at least two reasons for clearly separating the facts of a situation from your experience of the facts.

First, when you clearly give expression to your experience of a fact, you are communicating what the facts mean to you. This communicates to the other person how important it is to you and why it is important. Then your friend or partner knows how to respond in a way that is in line with your reasons for talking about it. If you casually mention that you met an old friend while out shopping (the fact), without adding whether or not you were excited, anxious, sad, or flooded with memories, your partner will not know how important it was to you and may respond without the degree of interest that is congruent with your experience. If you did not mention your experience, your partner might ask about it, and then he would know about it after you told him. But he might change the topic because he was thinking about something else and didn't stop to ponder if it was important or not to you. Tell him about your experience of the event and there will be no question about its importance.

Second, if you communicate your experience of a person or event as if it were fact, your friend or partner might become defensive or critical if it was not their experience. For example, if you tell your partner you were disappointed because she did not want to visit your mother, she may well be annoyed that you questioned her motives in declining your suggestion to visit without asking her first. The better plan is to simply ask why she doesn't want to visit your mother. If you think her reason might be only partly true and that she doesn't seem to want to visit your mother, express it as a question, rather than a certainty. Your statement "I'm wondering if you just don't enjoy visiting my mother very much" is likely to be met with much less defensiveness than if you said, "You never want to visit my mom anymore."

Your experience is simply your experience, and if you are open to reexperience an event based on what your friend tells you, your expression of it is not likely to create a problem in the relationship. If you speak as if your experience is fact, you are much more likely to elicit an angry, defensive response.

Exercise

Which of the following express experiences, facts, and experiences that are communicated as facts?

1. "I think you wanted to upset your brother." This communication relates to your experience.
2. "You wanted to upset your brother." This communication is of your experience but it is presented as a fact. You truly do not know if the person was motivated to upset his or her brother.
3. "You upset your brother." This communication is describing a fact—your brother is upset—without conveying any experience of the sibling's motives.

Addressing Conflicts

Michael and Nancy had been partners for three years. Their relationship was floundering and they were not sure why. Maybe they were wrong for each other. Maybe the other was losing interest in the relationship. Maybe the other was searching for something that he or she could not give. Or . . . maybe they both struggled with effective communication. Too often good—or even great—relationships end because of communication: its excesses, distortions, and deficiencies.

Example

Nancy was frustrated because Michael did not do his share of the household chores one Saturday morning. This was not the first time; he failed in his responsibilities more than he succeeded. Here are various ways they might have managed the situation poorly:

Scenario 1

NANCY: Would you *please* clean the living and dining rooms and the garage before going to Doug's for your coffee and sports "guy time." Once you're there, you forget everything and I'm not likely to see you till we're ready to head over to Mom's.

MICHAEL: I'm not that bad. I can't do anything without having my coffee anyway. I'll be back in an hour, tops.

NANCY: (*Frowning; in an annoyed tone.*) You always say that!

MICHAEL: (*With a smile and a lightness in his voice conveying little-boy charm.*) But this time I mean it, my love.

NANCY: Oh, go ahead. But please be back in an hour like you said. (*She smiles when he gives her a quick hug and kiss. When she hears the car pull out of the garage she swears to herself and forcefully throws the laundry she was gathering into the basket. When Michael returns over two hours later shortly before they were to head over to her mother's for lunch she barely talks to him. When they arrive, they both become engaged with her mother and with each* *other as if nothing had happened. The issue is not discussed until the next time—with similar words and results.)*

Scenario 2

NANCY: *(Hears Michael entering the kitchen while she is in the laundry room.)* Good morning!

MICHAEL: *(After getting some juice.)* I'm going over to Doug's for a bit. I'll be back in time to do my jobs before we go to your mother's.

NANCY: OK! Don't spend too much time there! *(When she hears the car pull out of the garage she swears to herself and forcefully throws the laundry . . .)*

Scenario 3

NANCY: *(Hears Michael entering the kitchen while she is in the laundry room. Enters the kitchen, yelling.)* You said you'd be getting up early so you'd be sure to get everything done in time for us to go to Mom's for lunch! You still have time but I don't want you to go over to Doug's!

MICHAEL: Good morning to you, too!

NANCY: I'm serious, Michael! You don't take this seriously!

MICHAEL: I just want some coffee first!

NANCY: Then have it here now! You got 15 minutes and then I want to hear the vacuum!

MICHAEL: You're on my back before I even wake up! If you want to hear the vacuum so bad then do it yourself!

NANCY: I'm on your back because you're not responsible enough to do it without my telling you to do it.

MICHAEL: Like it's the most important thing in the world! Spending a little time with my friend is more important to me than making sure that there is no speck of dust in the house!

NANCY: But not to me!

MICHAEL: You and the clean house police! I'm not going to deal with this right now!

NANCY: *(Yells at him as he heads to the door.)* You're such a child!
MICHAEL: And you're not my mother! *(Slams the door.)*

Scenario 4

Nancy leaves a note for Michael before leaving to meet a friend for breakfast and some shopping. The note says: "I'm with Julie and will be back before it's time to go to mom's. Since I did your chores last week, I left mine for you to do after you take care of yours. Don't forget the laundry after cleaning the kitchen and upstairs bathroom and our bedroom. See you later!"

When Michael gets up he reads the note, gets annoyed, and heads over to Doug's house. When Nancy gets home and sees that no chores were done, she goes to her mother's alone. Later that day they get together again for dinner, ignoring the unspoken, angry thoughts and emotions that each experienced toward the other that morning.

These examples involving Michael and Nancy demonstrate how partners often ineffectively communicate when they are faced with a problem. In the first example, Michael minimizes the conflict and Nancy agrees to go along, possibly hoping, again, that if she's "nice" about it, Michael will willingly do what she wants. In the second example they both deny that there's a problem, until Michael leaves and Nancy again shows her anger by throwing the laundry. In the first two examples the conflict is not addressed later in the day. In the third example the problem is immediately addressed with anger and defensiveness, escalating in turns. The anger could continue for hours afterward, but still the conflict would not be addressed. In the fourth example, the conflict is addressed by Nancy through her note, avoiding reciprocal communication, paying Michael back for not doing his share of the chores the week before, and leaving Michael free to engage in his passive-aggressive avoidance in return.

How might effective communication have addressed, and hopefully resolved, their problem with the weekly chores? The following sequence might have succeeded in avoiding the conflict in the first place, helped to address it quickly when it first appeared, and then helped to address a larger conflict that emerged later.

Step 1

Decide what is important to you and what you both need to do to achieve it. Be clear about what the goal is, how important it is to you both, and the specifics of what you each will do. Any differences of opinion need to be understood and accepted. If they are not resolved easily, then negotiations, compromises, and a plan that you both are comfortable with need to be developed. This early communication needs to be *thorough* (all the issues are covered), *reciprocal* (both of you express your thoughts and both of you listen to the thoughts of the other), and *clear* (both are clear on what you want).

When Michael and Nancy started living together they might have sat down to discuss how they would jointly manage the routine household responsibilities and chores. The best plan would have been for them to work on clarity regarding what the chores were (lists are still effective for this), what priority each gave each chore, how often it needed to be done, who would do it, and possibly when and how he or she would do it.

If Nancy believes that the bathroom should always be clean and Michael laughs because when he lived alone his place was always a mess, Nancy needs to be clear about whether she's fine with a mess or if neatness is an important issue for her. If their priorities are different about the bathroom, possibly Nancy would agree to be the one to clean the bathroom and Michael would agree to keep the living and dining rooms clean. If Michael laughs, saying that cleanliness is not important to him and he might not notice if the house is dirty, Nancy would need to clearly communicate how important it is to her and how important it is to her that Michael share the responsibility of keeping a clean house even if it is not a high priority for him. If Michael is reluctant to agree to do his share, regardless of how fair it is, he should clearly say so and then suggest another option to Nancy.

Step 2

After the plan is in place and being implemented, effective communication is valuable at the first sign that problems or conflicts are present. If one person believes that the other is not doing what he or she agreed to do, that person needs to understand why not. Maybe the other person has a reason and insists that things will be handled better in the future. Maybe the other person wants to renegotiate the agreement. Whatever the reason, the intent of this communication is to modify the original agreement if necessary to meet the goals of those in the relationship.

Staying with Nancy and Michael, let's assume that 2 weeks after the original agreement, Nancy notices that Michael has not once cleaned the living and dining rooms. She presents her observation to him and waits for his explanation for why he did not do this chore. Michael responds that he meant to do it but he just hadn't thought of it and the few times he did remember, he put off this chore to do something else that he enjoyed. Nancy clearly states how important a clean house is to her and how important it also is that he do his share of keeping it clean. Michael understands and agrees to do his share. They explore what he or they could do to be sure that this is accomplished. Michael decides that if he does it at the same time every week, he will accept the responsibility and not put it off. He chooses Saturday morning, and Nancy says she will do her share as well to help him remember; that way they can plan to do something that's mutually agreeable afterward.

Step 3

If the problem continues in spite of the original discussion and the plan to resolve it, it needs to be explored again, possibly at a deeper level. Now this issue that needs to be explored is not the original problem (that the living and dining rooms were not being cleaned), but rather the fact that what was agreed to is not being carried out.

After the second discussion there should have been no doubt in Michael's mind how important it was to Nancy that he clean the rooms as he said he would—now twice. The issue now is why he does not follow through on his commitments to Nancy when he knows that it is important to her. Again, the communication must be thorough, reciprocal, and clear.

It has been 5 weeks since the last communication and Michael has cleaned the rooms only twice, though Nancy had been cleaning her share of the house at the same time that Michael had said that he would be cleaning. He had been home, though he went to visit his friend Doug, before doing the cleaning.

NANCY: Michael, I'd like to talk now about you not doing your share of the cleaning on a consistent basis. Since we originally talked about it 7 weeks ago, you've done it only twice.

MICHAEL: I know. I need to do it more often like I said that I would.

NANCY: You said that last time, Michael, and that's what I don't understand. I was clear about how important this was to me and you were clear in your commitment to do it. Now I'm not sure how seriously you take my requests or how much you really listen to me about what's important to me. And I'm beginning to wonder how seriously you take the commitments that you make to me.

MICHAEL: We're only talking about cleaning the living and dining rooms. This doesn't seem important enough to be all concerned about.

NANCY: It's more than clean rooms, Michael. It's about whether something that's important to me will be remembered by you. And it's about whether or not you keep the commitments that you make to me, no matter what they are. Those are very important issues to me, Michael, and, I believe, to the health of our relationship.

MICHAEL: I didn't realize it would be that important to you whether I cleaned the rooms.

NANCY: Then I have to be more clear. What's important to me is that you listen when I tell you that something's important to me and that when you tell me you'll do something that's important to me, I know that you'll do it. Cleaning the rooms is no longer the important issue. Being able to trust that you'll listen and that you'll keep your word to me is much more important.

MICHAEL: This time I hear you. I really do. I'm sorry I didn't follow through and I see that I have to do so when I say I will. I can honestly say that I will do so from here on out—I will truly listen to what you're saying and I'll keep my word when I make a commitment to you. I know that you listen and I can count on your doing what you say. You deserve the same from me. I'm sorry.

NANCY: Thank you, Michael. I'm really glad we addressed this and you're taking it seriously.

KEY 7

TINKER AND REPAIR

Healthy relationships have problems. People in healthy relationships make mistakes. The honeymoon ends. We know that, right? Yes, but the question is, what do we do when the mistakes and problems and the light of day arrive? If at the first sign of these realities we conclude that the relationship itself was a mistake and we run, we are not likely to ever experience a healthy relationship. If at the next sign of these realities we hide our head in the sand, our relationship is not likely to generate true safety and development. If these realities take on an exaggerated life of their own, we are likely to lose sight of the healthy aspects of our relationship.

We may be tempted to focus on what is lovely, enjoyable, and satisfying in our relationships and not pay enough attention to mistakes and problems, which we need to do if they are to be managed and reduced. We need to face the unpleasant features of our relationships if we are to nourish the most meaningful elements. Being desperate to always agree on everything, we are likely to move into a fantasy relationship that lacks real health. So we need to face the difficulties, repair the relationship when necessary, and build our healthy relationship on true human realities.

As researchers studied attachment they came to realize that securely attached infants did not have parents who perfectly anticipated and responded to their every need as soon as it was expressed. In fact, when parents did obsessively focus on their child's every desire so that their child would not feel any distress or unhappiness, those children tended to be anxiously attached. Children with attachment security tended to have parents who were available, sensitive, and responsive while also making mistakes, noticing in their infant's response that the behavior was a mistake, and then modifying the behavior until they got it right and the relationship was repaired.[1] This became known as "interactive repair" among attachment researchers and was quickly seen as central in facilitating attachment security. The secure infant developed trust in knowing that the parent would get it right after making a mistake, would return after a separation, and would reconnect after a conflict.

Yes, in your attachment relationships, mistakes will happen, as will separations, conflicts, misunderstandings, and times when your partner simply does not notice something that was important to you. Or you do not notice something that was important to him or her. In the early stages of your relationship you may not notice these relationship "breaks" because of the positive experience of intimacy that you habitually feel. Or you may choose not to address it for fear that the conflict might prematurely hurt the relationship. And you convince yourself that the problem was not that important anyway. When you begin to notice and address your problems, mistakes, differences, and misunderstandings, you are entering a deeper, more realistic stage in the development of your relationship. You are trusting that the problem will not end the relationship.

So make mistakes, please. Not deliberately—they will happen without your forcing them. But when you do make mistakes, when you do differ or misunderstand, then address these instances! Your relationship will deepen and with each act of repair you will be able to better handle future problems.

A few years ago, in my role as a therapist I saw a couple who had drifted apart and lived with habitual tension and isolation. The man in the relationship stubbornly avoided all conflicts. When his

---

1. E. Tronick, *The neurobehavioral and social-emotional development of infants and children* (New York: W. W. Norton, 2007).

partner tried to address them he became withdrawn and passive, finally walking away. As this pattern was addressed in treatment, eventually his partner said, "You say that you love me but I don't experience it. If you love me, you have to be willing to argue with me!" This direct statement contradicted all of the man's attachment learning that he had obtained from his parents. They had wanted a good boy who not only obeyed but never even disagreed with them. He thought that to show his love for his parents he had to always agree with them and do what they wanted. He was stunned by his partner's exclamation that she needed him to argue with her to help her to experience his love.

This chapter focuses on repairing the inevitable problems that occur in all intimate relationships. Healthy relationships are not free of the various breaks mentioned above. In healthy relationships the partners accept the breaks, address them, and tinker with them, and the relationship is repeatedly repaired. When this is done well, your relationship will be stronger.

Example

Thomas was a successful lawyer who had built his group practice with his eye on having his son join him one day. Tim knew how important it was to his father that he enter the practice and when he was young, he felt proud that his dad wanted him to work with him. He even played at being a lawyer in his childhood games. When he attended university he worked during the summers at his father's firm. Everything moved along as planned and he applied to law school and was accepted.

Tim spent the summer before he started school fighting fires with some friends in the Western mountains. He fell in love with the land, especially the mountains, and the relaxed way of life. He decided to stay, work in the ski resorts in the winter, and delay law school. It was hard telling his dad, and harder too was his father's reaction. His father announced that Tim had betrayed him, that he was ungrateful and selfish and immature. Tim was stunned and went back to the mountains in confusion and anger. He never did go to law school.

He visited home regularly, mostly to see his mom, his sisters, and his friends from the past. He and his father were civil, formal, and distant. His being a lawyer was never discussed; also not discussed was Tim's career managing a pub and restaurant and giving ski lessons in a small city in Colorado that he had fallen in love with.

Too often, much too often, situations such as that just described concerning Thomas and Tim occur. The relationship is never the same afterward. This happens in relationships between parent and child and between partners. Somehow, the conflict becomes larger than the relationship. The conflict then ends the relationship, or at least the relationship that gives meaning and joy to those who had been close to each other. Somehow the issue that led to the conflict takes on tremendous meaning to at least one person in the relationship.

In the example given above, Thomas was deeply committed to his career while at the same time he experienced a strong love for his son. His love for Tim connected very easily—in his mind—with his passion for being a lawyer. He saw his strong encouragement and practical support for Tim's entering his practice as evidence of his love for his son and his son's love for him. His gift to his son—a fast track to a successful law practice—represented his love for his son; his son's following this path toward being a lawyer in his father's practice represented his son's love for him. When Tim chose to follow another path—life in a small Western town providing ski lessons and managing a pub—Thomas experienced that choice as a rejection of him, as a lack of love in return for all that he had given Tim. In this situation, for Thomas, Tim's career choice to be a lawyer became the foundation of their relationship, while for Tim, choosing to live in the West with more relaxed goals, though this might be disappointing for his dad, was simply his own choice for his career and did not convey any meaning about his love for his dad. Tim never dreamed that in choosing to work out West he would cause a major problem in his relationship with his father.

Imagine if, when Thomas discovered that Tim was planning to remain in the West and not pursue law school, he initiated the following conversation with his son:

THOMAS: I thought you were definitely going to law school. You seemed to be so interested in law as your career and so committed to pursuing it. I've really been looking forward to your being a lawyer and working with me someday.

TIM: I know, Dad. And I know how much you were looking forward to my joining the practice. I'm sorry for causing you so much disappointment. I guess I really had never thought about a life like I had this summer. I felt so free, so happy, and I just want to stay and see where it leads me. I never felt this way before—like I'm more alive than I ever knew was possible. I feel that I just have to give this a try. If it doesn't work out and I want to go back to law, then so be it. I will have found out for myself that what seems to be so special to me now won't last. But I have to find out for myself, Dad, I really do.

THOMAS: I hear you, son. And yes, I am disappointed. I've been thinking for a long time about you and me working together. That my dream would be your dream. But if it isn't for you, Tim, it isn't for you. You have to find out for yourself, and whatever you decide, I'll support you.

TIM: Thanks, Dad. I knew you'd be there for me, no matter what. And I'm sorry I've hurt you by giving up law, at least for now.

THOMAS: Yes, I'm hurt, but I'd be more hurt if you didn't love law the way I do. You need to find your passion, Tim.

TIM: Thanks, Dad. I love you.

THOMAS: And I love you, Tim. Whether you're a lawyer or a forest ranger or a bartender. That doesn't matter.

People in relationships need to be able to repair whatever conflicts emerge if the relationships are to become truly meaningful and lasting. Repairing conflicts enables relationships to attain depth and value while maintaining their for-better-or-worse quality. Avoiding conflicts may enable a relationship to continue but at the price of depth and meaning. Avoiding conflicts leads to a more polite but superficial relationship, one more suited to acquaintances or casual friends. If you want a meaningful relationship, you need to be willing to accept conflict and engage in relationship repair.

In this chapter I break out the fundamental points about relationship tinkering and repairing that you should keep in mind.

Decide If the Relationship Is More Important Than the Conflict

Sometimes in the heat of the moment, the here-and-now conflict makes us forget the importance of our relationship with our friend or partner. Then we say or do things that hurt the relationship much more than the original conflict itself has hurt it. If we hold on to the big picture of the place of the relationship in our lives, we are more likely to resolve the conflict rather than compound it.

When the conflict seems to be larger than the relationship, you might ask if it is because you're giving it a larger meaning than it deserves. If your partner doesn't share with you something that's bothering him or her, does that really show unwillingness to rely on you and a lack of value for your views? Or might it mean that your partner approaches difficulties differently, wanting to think things through on his or her own before expressing his or her thoughts to you or to anyone? Differences in personalities or problem-solving habits do not necessarily represent how important your relationship is to your partner.

Remember the Importance of the Relationship

When you are able to experience how important your relationship is to both you and your partner, you will be more likely to keep in mind that any conflict is not too much for the relationship to manage. When the positive in your relationship is clear, strong, and meaningful, the negative will have a context that makes it easier to address and resolve.

Conflicts seem worse when the reasons for the relationship in the first place—sharing ideas and interests, enjoyment, passion, laughter, developing plans and goals together—are forgotten or taken for granted. Don't forget that your relationship is a big part of your life. When you remember its value to you, you will be more impelled to work toward resolving any conflict that emerges.

Remember That Assigning Blame Is Counterproductive

Conflicts come and go. You and your partner have two different perspectives regardless of how strong your relationship is. If you both have only one perspective, the relationship has probably developed at the expense of the need for autonomy that you both have. Two perspectives are simply that. It's unlikely that one is right and the other wrong. Simply accepting that you and your partner see something differently, without trying to decide who is right and who is wrong, will enable you both to address a difference if it seems important to do so, without eliciting a defensive attitude that comes from the need to be right.

Yes, if you start from a position that you and your partner have two positions, both equally valid, then you are more likely to approach the conflict in an open and engaged manner, without defensiveness—which will mean that your partner is less likely to be defensive as well. If that is the case, the conflict is much more likely to lead to something that works for you both rather than there being a "winner" and a "loser." In your important relationships, if you win and your friend or partner loses, then you both lose.

Don't Deny or Avoid: Address the Conflict

You might think, the relationship is important and the conflict is not that important, so why not just overlook the conflict and carry on with your life together? This is a fine idea if it truly is not that important, if it happened because you got up on the wrong side of the bed, or your partner did. However, if the conflict does not go away, then trying to overlook it will cause much more damage to your relationship than would be caused by the temporary stress of addressing it. As conflicts emerge and are not addressed, you are likely to find yourself or your partner avoiding many events, topics, or activities that you might share, in order to prevent possible dangers that seem to be emerging throughout your daily life. You then notice that you have less and less to share or do together. You also notice that you are vigilant in your life together for fear of tripping over something that might be stressful for your relationship.

You might ask why you tend to avoid or deny conflicts. Various reasons come to mind:

> You might feel insecure about the strength and commitment of the relationship. So you avoid conflicts for fear that they will be too much for the relationship to handle.
>
> You might be uncomfortable with anger and so avoid any situation that might create that emotion. When you or your partner expresses anger, it tends to become very intense and lead to one of you saying things that you don't really mean. You might make threats in the heat of the moment and find yourself locked into consequences that you do not really want.
>
> When you begin to address a conflict you tend to lose your way. One thing leads to the next and soon you are talking about every difference that you have, differences that have simmered for months or years.
>
> You have trouble asserting yourself when you think your partner might disagree with you. You confuse assertiveness with selfishness. You tend to automatically think that what your partner wants is more valid than what you want.

You might have a dismissive attachment style which would suggest that you tend to downplay both emotion and relationships in your life and so not exert the needed energy to manage situations that touch on either of those.

Don't Endlessly Replay Conflict

The opposite of denying or minimizing conflicts in your relationships is to constantly dwell on the conflicts and experience them again and again, without an end in sight. Whereas avoiding conflicts might suggest a dismissive attachment style, conflicts being central to your relationships might suggest a preoccupied attachment style.

You might ask why you tend to replay your conflicts over and over. Various reasons come to mind:

While you are able to acknowledge your conflicts, when they begin you tend to have difficulty discussing them sufficiently so as to successfully find a resolution. The stress of communicating about the conflict leads to ending the discussion prematurely.

You might find that when you focus on a conflict that you are having with your partner, there is an emotional vibrancy to the relationship that does not exist outside your conflicts. The task then is to find ways to bring other forms of emotional intensity to your relationships.

You, your partner, or both have a strong need to be right rather than to resolve the conflict.

You, your partner, or both tend to have trouble truly listening to the perspective of the other. Your defensive stance makes it hard to be open and engaged in the discussion.

You feel unsure in your relationships if you cannot achieve complete agreement on what you and your partner think and feel and give priority to. You have trouble accepting the place of differences in your relationships.

Remember That Behavior Has More Than One Meaning

Assuming that you know the reason behind a behavior can often lead to a conflict that was never intended in the first place. You might be certain that your partner forgot her commitment to call you, or worse yet, remembered but did not feel like contacting you, so she didn't bother. You were preparing to express your anger when you saw her that evening. Before you had a chance she told you that she had spent most of the day with her best friend in the emergency room. Your anger was tied to what you assumed were negative motives for her not calling you more than her not calling you itself. Why not forget your emotional response to her behavior until you know her reason for it?

Address One Conflict at a Time

When you have a conflict, address it then, not next month or next year. If you have a conflict and don't address it in a timely manner, it might be best to simply forget it. If you bring it up a month later, chances are your memory of it will have drifted in one direction and your partner's memory of it in another direction. The odds will probably be poor that you agree enough on what happened and what the circumstances were that led to it happening. It's best to address the conflict as soon as your emotions are regulated enough for you to be able to reflect on what's bothering you and your friend's emotions appear to be similarly in check. At that time your emotions will guide your reflecting on the event and keep you focused on the immediate situation. If you wait too long, your reflecting might drift into other areas and become too abstract rather than tied to the immediate, concrete experience.

When you have a conflict, address it by itself, not in combination with five other conflicts. When you have a grab bag of things in your relationship with your partner that you are annoyed about, you may join them in such a way that none of them is adequately addressed and the combination leaves you and your partner defensive and frustrated. If you bring up five conflicts at once, your partner will focus on the one that is your weakest argument or is the least important to you. Then the most important one will be forgotten and not resolved. At the same time your partner will sense that you are not satisfied with anything about him and he will most likely become discouraged with the apparent hopelessness of ever being able to please you.

Mistakes Happen: Say You're Sorry. Period.

When you enter a healthy relationship you don't make a promise to never make a mistake, to never be slightly selfish, insensitive, or nonobservant. You're human and you'll make mistakes at times with your friend or partner. So make them, acknowledge them, and say you're sorry. There is a saying: "Love means never having to say you're sorry." I strongly disagree with that. Saying that you're sorry shows an awareness that you hurt or may have hurt your friend along with a readiness to express regret and to commit to repairing your relationship. Your friend is important to you. You do experience remorse for what you did and you are motivated not to do it again.

If you avoid admitting to mistakes on a regular basis, you may be struggling with shame—as if mistakes mean that there's something wrong with you! Rather than doing something insensitive, you are insensitive. Rather than doing something that was too self-centered, you are self-centered. If you feel shame over your action you are less likely to admit to it. Rather, you will have excuses for it, even blame your friend for his part in your behavior, or minimize its importance. Then if he doesn't immediately forgive you, you become annoyed with him for not letting it go. All those actions are likely to contain a strong element of shame. It's much better to admit that you made a mistake than to run from it in shame.

You may be willing to say that you're sorry and then insist on giving the reasons for your misdeed. You explain that you want your friend to understand why you made the mistake so she will not misread your motives or think that what you did represents more than it does. However, when you need to give your reasons, most likely your friend will hear them as excuses. By providing the reasons for your mistake you're seeking to be held less accountable for what you did. Thus, this suggestion: Say you're sorry. Period. You are accountable. Your friend must now decide what your mistake means with regard to your ongoing relationship. If she wants to know more about the context in which you made your mistake, she will ask you. If you volunteer your reasons, most likely you will be perceived as simply providing an excuse.

Example

John was having a hard day. He was stuck in traffic; he forgot a commitment at work, possibly costing his company a client; he spilled coffee on his new shirt; and he seemed to have lost his cell phone. When he got home that night he yelled at Sandy for leaving her car in the driveway, he complained that this was the third time this week they had had leftovers, and he turned on the TV while she was in the middle of telling him about something interesting that had happened to her that day.

Scenario 1

SANDY: John, you've been snapping at me ever since you walked in the door. And now you're ignoring me. I'm getting upset with how you're treating me.

JOHN: I'm sorry, but if you knew how hard my day was maybe you wouldn't complain that I've not been in the best mood. Nothing went right today.

SANDY: How am I supposed to know that when you don't tell me?

JOHN: OK, I'm sorry. But I really had a hard day. I think if you knew, you would understand.

SANDY: Understand why you decided to give me a hard day too?

While John may be correct in that he would not be so irritable with his partner if he had not had such a difficult day at work,
he is not correct in combining the two when confronted by Sandy over his behavior. In so doing, he seems to be justifying his
behavior while at the same time turning the focus away from
Sandy's distress toward his own. In responding to her distress, his
focus would have been better received if he had acknowledged
that he had caused the distress and then apologized for what he
had done. He is truly sorry. Period. Then Sandy would decide
where to go next in their dialogue. She may want to finish her
story. She may want to know why he was being harsh with her.
She may want to speak about his irritability with her further if
she believes that it represents a developing pattern of behavior
toward her.

Scenario 2

SANDY: John, you've been snapping at me ever since you walked
in the door. And now you're ignoring me. I'm getting upset with
how you're treating me.

JOHN: (*Stares at the TV for 5 seconds and then turns it off.*) I'm
sorry, Sandy. You're right. I haven't treated you very well this evening and I really am sorry.

SANDY: I'm glad to hear that.

JOHN: Would you give me another chance and tell me what happened at work today?

SANDY: Thanks, John. I appreciate that. But before I tell you,
would you tell me what's going on with you? Something really
seems to be on your mind.

JOHN: Sure, honey. I think I should have told you when I walked
in the door rather than taking it out on you. Well, just about everything went wrong that could go wrong. . . .

In this scenario, John reflects for a moment and inhibits any
tendency to become defensive. Sandy's assertive comment is accurate. Knowing that, his primary motive is to repair the relationship and the best way to do that seemed to be to say that he was

sorry and to mean what he said. Sandy then responds by accepting his apology and then initiating the discussion about possible reasons—not excuses—for his behavior. (Knowing the reason helps us understand the cause for the behavior that he is accountable for, and helps prevent it from happening again. An excuse says that one is not accountable for his behavior.)

By becoming adept at tinkering and repairing your relationship in response to the various troubles and challenges that are certain to come, you will find greater safety and satisfaction, comfort and joy. When conflicts are seen as an opportunity to strengthen your relationship rather than as a risk to its durability, you are likely to have fewer conflicts, and when they emerge, they will simply be seen as a necessary part of your relationship. I am not suggesting that you embrace them or even welcome them, but simply that you accept them and begin to tinker rather than tremble.

So, to summarize, remember these important, conflict-preventing tips:

- Before acting on your guess about the meaning of your partner's behavior, consider alternative reasons why he might have done what he did.
- Keep your guess about the meaning of his behavior tentative until you ask him about it.
- Ask him openly about his behavior without a judgmental attitude.
- Truly listen to what he says about his reasons for his behavior.
- If your concerns about his behavior remain, address them, conveying clearly why you were troubled by his behavior.
- Listen to his response to your concerns, being open to his perspective.
- If you still have concerns, express them openly. Remember that you have two perspectives and that you are not necessarily "right," nor is he "wrong."
- If differences continue, commit to a way forward that meets the needs of both of you, acknowledging that your relationship is important to you both.

KEY 8

BALANCE AUTONOMY
WITH INTIMACY

Autonomous attachment relationships are actually the relationships that provide the greatest safety, that are the most satisfying, and that facilitate the development of both autonomy and intimacy. Autonomous attachments provide safety because they ensure that individuals do not ask too much or too little from relationships. If the responsibility of a relationship is to provide most of the meaning and joy that exists in your life, it will fail. If your life contains few meaningful relationships, their meaning and joy are likely to be limited. When you bring a way of living described as autonomous to your relationships, your relationships and your independent interests and pursuits both thrive.

What is essential, then, is creating and keeping a vibrant balance between autonomy and intimacy in your life. When such a balance is achieved, you will find that you have more energy and interest in both. Your relationships and independent interests will be deeper and richer, as will those of your partner and close friends. Autonomy and intimacy are not in competition with each other—each supports and enhances the value of the other. Here are some important insights to keep in mind to achieve this balance.

The Need for Autonomy in a Developing Relationship

Throughout this book I have encouraged you to think about what makes you unique. The discussion has included your attachment history, woven into your autobiography. It has also included the complementary skills and activities of reflecting and feeling and then bringing them together in clear nonverbal and verbal communication. It also most certainly has included developing and repairing your relationships so they are well maintained. Taking all this together helps you give expression to all the qualities of your inner life that are important to you, through your daily activities, pursuits, and dreams. This comprehensive pattern gives rise to your autonomy—the living expression of all that makes you who you are as you live your life in the present while being aware of your hopes for the future.

Your sense of autonomy encompasses your sense of agency, which refers to your ability to seek and attain your goals. You are not a passive recipient of your life; you are active in creating it. Your autonomy is a part of the nature of your relationships and what they bring to the rest of your life. However, if your relationships define the actions and meanings of your life, your autonomy begins to wither and you have less to bring to those with whom you relate. And they begin to wither too.

Example

Blake had been looking for a woman like Sherrie for quite some time, ever since his relationship with Kim ended abruptly almost three years before. Now 32, Blake had felt empty and without a sense of direction since Kim. Things that he generally looked forward to—his photography, movies, and antiques—did not hold much meaning. But since he had met Sherrie, they were alive for him again. Sherrie had such energy, she was so positive about everything, and she enjoyed what she did. On top of this, she was successful, attractive, and creative. What more could he ask for? Blake was happy, happier than he could remember ever having been with Kim or, for that matter, with Anne, Rochelle, or Jeannette.

The word *happiness* summed up the excitement and joy Blake felt when he was with Sherrie, as well as when he thought of seeing her and was counting the hours till he did. Of course, he also felt happy when going through a new batch of photos he'd taken after spending a weekend outdoors searching for the right light and composition. But that happiness was not as intense, predictable, or important to him as when he was with Sherrie. For the past 18 months he had maintained a routine of devoting the first weekend of the month to photography. He would look forward to it, carefully plan his trip, check his equipment, and spend the following week studying his photographs and deciding which ones were worthy of enhancement, cropping, and maybe even printing. Of course every month did not yield a photo to frame, but that did not matter. However, this month he spent the first weekend wandering around the city with Sherrie. He even forgot that it was his photography weekend until Sherrie told him that she was surprised to get his phone call about spending the weekend with her. She thought that he would be going somewhere with his camera!

They had been going out together for two months when Sherrie said she would be going to visit her family the next weekend, so she would not be seeing him then. Blake was disappointed that she did not invite him to go along, but he understood. It was probably too soon. She'd ask him next time. But 2 weeks later he started to feel anxious. He asked her to go with him to an art exhibit and she reminded him that it was his weekend for photography. He said he'd rather spend it with her, but she insisted that he stick to his routine, saying she knew it was very important to him. At first he thought her words were a sign of her sensitivity toward him and what was important to him. But then he asked her again to spend that weekend with him—and she refused. She said she had made plans to spend some time with a friend, thinking that he would be devoting himself to his photography. He felt anxiety, and then he was annoyed. Why didn't she ask him first? Why shouldn't he decide how he wanted to spend his weekend? She admitted that she had not made a strong commitment to her friend. So why didn't she want to spend it with him, since he was free?

Blake began to obsess about Sherrie's possible motives and his suppositions were not reassuring. Maybe she was losing interest in him. Maybe he was too possessive. Maybe she had met someone else. Maybe she never did like him as much as he thought that she did. Maybe she just was not interested in making a commitment to him . . . or to anyone. He remembered that he had started to have similar worries before his relationship with Kim ended. And his doubts had proved to be well founded. It was happening again, wasn't it?

Yes, it did happen again. Sherrie noticed Blake's annoyance with her. But what bothered her most was that it seemed to linger. And then he seemed to want her to commit to spending time with him 2 or 3 weeks in advance. His calls and texts seemed to be getting more frequent and when she was not available to respond quickly, he didn't wait but sent another one. And she could sense his frustration in those subsequent messages. So Sherrie began to pull away, just a bit. She told Blake that she liked spending time with him, but she would like to slow it down a bit. She said she hoped he would grant her request because she really did like him. But he only seemed to be more disappointed, more frustrated; and if anything, he wanted to spend even more time with her. So she became more firm and more insistent that in their relationship he needed to let her set a pace she was comfortable with. He demanded angrily, "Why is it always about what you want! Why isn't what I want important too!" She didn't know what to say. She didn't know who Blake was. Or maybe now she did. She had tears in her eyes when she ended the relationship—tears over what she had imagined it might become and now knew it never would.

What happened? Blake's happiness, his delight, his excitement, his sense of being alive—all were real. They were intense; they were so enjoyable to experience! And he knew that Sherrie was feeling the same things when she was with him! She had all the qualities he was looking for! Why did she change her mind? What happened?

The positive emotions that Blake experienced in his photography, antiques, and movies all faded away when he met Sherrie. All his positive emotions became associated with activities he did with her. He felt that without the relationship, his emotional life had seemed barren. What gave him his sense of autonomy seemed to hold little meaning for him. Only his relationship with Sherrie seemed to hold meaning

Remember from the table in Key 1 that those who show features of secure attachment in childhood are considered to manifest autonomous attachment in adulthood? Secure and autonomous—these appear to be opposing qualities. So why are they said to represent the same characteristics, one as applied to children and the other to adults? The reason is that when children demonstrate secure attachment they are well on their way to functioning independently in many situations. Such children, when they are safe within a relationship with the primary person they have an attachment to, are learning to face the challenges and opportunities of the world by relying on their inner resources. Securely attached children are both safe to explore and competent in exploring their world. They are honing their confidence in their abilities apart from their primary attachment person while at the same time developing their own unique interests and ideas. They are developing their sense of autonomy. Contrary to what the word *attachment* might conjure up, attachment security does not lead to dependency but, rather, to the ability to blend independence and dependence, according to the needs and options that arise in the immediate situation. Children are developing the ability to have deep satisfaction, meaning, and interests both when alone and in a relationship with an important friend. They do not sacrifice one for the other.

This balance did not exist for Blake. When he was in a relationship that had the potential to become more serious, he was unable to preserve his sense of meaning and enjoyment that came from his autonomous interests and activities. His sense of being alive and experiencing excitement, joy, and fulfillment seemed, for Blake, to exist only during the intimacy of the early stages of an important relationship. Ideally, once the honeymoon period of getting to know each other wore off, he would be able to maintain a balance between Sherrie and his interest in photography and antiques and achieve satisfaction in both.

In light of his increasing efforts to control Sherrie and his struggle to accept her autonomy, however, it seems he could not achieve that balance. Rather, because he was not able to have control over her interests and behavior—bring about her dependency on him—he became dissatisfied with her. If she became increasingly dependent, for Blake she would begin to exhibit fewer of the characteristics that had attracted him in the first place and he would tire of her. Or if she fought to retain some independence, he would take that as a sign that she did not deeply love him. Either way, he probably would begin to seek another partner.

Blake manifested a preoccupied attachment pattern; he was prepared to sacrifice his sense of autonomy in order to have an intimate relationship. His emotions toward Sherrie were intense, overwhelming the quieter emotions associated with his interests and his overall reflective abilities. He could not rest while apart from her, even when pursuing things that had been important to him for years.

Strategies for Maintaining Autonomy

If you find yourself sacrificing your sense of autonomy and focusing intensely on your relationships, it is probable that you are showing signs of a preoccupied attachment style. If you wish to develop and preserve your autonomy, there is value in knowing who you are and knowing the features of who you are that are central to your sense of what, for you, makes up a well-lived life.

Beginning a Journal About Who You Are

It is helpful to take an inventory of the bits of yourself that constitute your most important features. Understanding the unique, interwoven patterns of these bits will help you describe what makes you autonomous. I would suggest that you get pen and paper and take the time to describe to yourself the special experiences and features that make you, you. The following lists will help you do so.

Looking to the Past

- Family roots and notable characters
- Local community and school with their unique challenges and opportunities
- Peer relationships and activities that filled your day and created unique experiences
- Particular talents, interests, habits, and obligations: how they filled your mind and heart
- The draw of the future from childhood through adolescence into the stages of adulthood, your hopes and dreams

Looking at the Present

- Work: meaning, skills required, time involved, financial benefits
- Love: meaning, depth, breadth, continuity, experiences they bring to your life
- Play: priorities for your free time, benefits, relaxation, creativity, positive addictions
- Maintaining your life: caring for your mind and body (curiosity and learning, exercise and diet, habits—healthy and not), learning from mistakes, challenges, opportunities
- The big picture: the totality of your well-lived life

Looking to the Future

- What you want the present to look like in 10, 20, 30 years
- Plans to attain your goals and confidence in your plans
- What you want to pass on to others; which others in particular

- Your spirituality and soul mates
- Thoughts about death

If you were to keep a journal about yourself that included these features, it would extend your autobiography from the past into your present and future. You would have a sense of how your past and future influence your present and how your present—when you are fully, mindfully present in what you are now experiencing—enables your past and future to remain vibrant. Rest assured that your journal will be unique. What you have written deserves to be valued and tended to.

Using Your Journal

Revisit your journal of who you are and reflect on what kind of relationship might add to a particular feature, rather than simply how the relationship might place limits on it. Bringing a relationship into features of your autonomy may enrich them and make them more complex. Your interest in traveling may well be enhanced if your partner also likes to travel. Even if she doesn't, if she is interested in hearing about your travels—if you have someone to share your adventures with upon returning home—you are likely to enjoy them more.

Strive to maintain your personal interests and meaningful habits at the outset when embarking on a new relationship. Ensure that the blocks of time that you have devoted to them in the past are still available. This will ensure that you will not rely too much on the other person for your enjoyment and will also help you to know if the other person will support your desire to maintain some interests and solitary time that are important to you.

If you value your autonomy you will strive to ensure that it is given sufficient attention, so that it is not devalued at the beginning of a new relationship. You will have confidence that the relationship will not be harmed by your attention to what makes you unique and what gives you a reason for getting out of bed in the morning, with enthusiasm and curiosity about what lies ahead.

Your autonomy and the time and energy you devote to the activities through which you exercise it do not detract from your developing relationship but rather enhance it.

When Blake began to give up his photography and his interest in antiques and movies when he began his relationship with Sherrie, she was rightfully concerned. Her concern grew when he also began to urge her to give up her independent interests and the time she spent with her family and friends without him. What made him unique—his autonomous interests and activities—were central to her attraction to him. As he began to set them aside for her, he began to have less to offer the relationship. Rather than wanting to contribute his sense of autonomy to the relationship, he wanted to set it aside and live for the relationship. Sherrie knew that she could not be the source of Blake's happiness; nor did she want to be. She wanted to share with him what made her unique and have him share with her what made him unique. She did not want to set aside those features of both of them in order to live in a hothouse where only their relationship was valued.

While it is understandable and even desirable to spend extra time with your new friend or potential partner at the early stage of a relationship, it is not wise to set everything aside and focus only on the relationship itself. It is tempting to do that because of the insecurity that comes from not knowing if the relationship will deepen and be lasting. That creates an urge to push it along, to remove the uncertainty through spending extra time together, sharing and doing things together as much as possible to discover if this is the right person for you. However, such knowledge is not as reliable as you want to believe it is. Relationships need time to evolve and they set their own pace. They need time to simmer, for you to add to their ingredients one at a time.

Setting aside your autonomous interests and preferences will give a distorted view of the future after you have made a commitment to each other. Once you are certain that this is the right person, and the other person agrees and is content with you as well, then you may have the opposite problem—taking each other for granted.

Bringing the other—and his or her interests, values, personality, and dreams, those things that make up her sense of autonomy—alongside you in a way that accommodates your autonomy is likely to add to both your lives, without diminishing the core of either of them.

Integrate Relationships into Your Life

Just as it is wise for you to maintain your autonomy when you pursue relationships, it is equally important to allow room for the development of relationships in your life as you maintain your autonomy. Relationships need not hinder your sense of autonomy if you experience yourself as being a person who wants, is capable of, and is committed to participating in healthy relationships throughout your life. When your sense of autonomy includes the development of a coherent life story and reflective and emotional competence as well as excellent communication skills and the ability to establish and repair reciprocal relationships, then healthy relationships are likely to flourish. If you are tempted to think that your life would be easier if you avoided the give-and-take of relationships and the uncertainties of emotions (if you tend toward a dismissive attachment style), remember that easier does not often mean more fulfilling and meaningful. Integrating relationships into your sense of autonomy may well bring about much greater vibrancy and purpose in your life.

Example

Trista had always done well in school, graduating from her university near the top of her class. So she was not surprised to find herself doing well in her first job after college, at a large company in Chicago. Within 6 months she was told that her position was secure. Within 2 years she was given a major promotion in her department and within 7 years she was asked to manage that department. Turning 30, she not only greatly enjoyed her career; she felt that her future was more than assured.

Trista's energy was not restricted to her career. She looked fit and she was. Her diet and exercise regimen could have come right out of a wellness magazine. Her free time was highly satisfying. She liked traveling, music and art, skiing and snorkeling. Trista had a full life and much to offer in her friendships and in a relationship with a potential partner.

As she turned 30 Trista realized that she had had many enjoyable relationships in her life with available men. They usually lasted only a number of months, however, though a few had lasted more than a year. Generally she was the one who ended the relationship. She didn't think much about why this was, but at the time when she was ending it, her reasons seemed valid.

When she met Anthony she hoped that this relationship might lead to a long-term commitment. He seemed to have all the qualities she found attractive in a partner—he was friendly and considerate, successful and good-looking, an excellent skier, with a sense of adventure. She also felt that at her age, she would like to begin to think about settling down.

The first several months seemed to go well. They shared so many interests that there always seemed to be something they both wanted to do. When they wanted different things they were good at working out compromises that neither seemed to resent. Anthony tended to want to talk about their relationship more than Trista did, just as he shared more about his life and upbringing than she did about hers. She didn't see much point in talking about the past. Emotions were also hard for her to talk about. She felt exposed and vulnerable when she did—and these were two emotions she did not like to experience.

It was the differences in how Trista and Anthony approached their emotional lives that seemed to create the first major problems in their relationship. Anthony would become disappointed that Trista did not share with him things that might be bothering her at her work or in her family. He also sensed that she was not

really interested in his hopes and dreams, worries and doubts—unless he wanted a practical suggestion from her. He could rely on her for practical suggestions but not that much for emotional support and companionship.

When Anthony told her one weekend that he thought their relationship was not going anywhere and that they should see other people, Trista was hurt and then angry. She had not seen the break-up coming. She didn't see anything wrong with their relationship and it seemed to her that he had misled her or was asking for too much. After a few weeks, Trista decided that she was better off without Anthony. She began to think of examples where he was too needy. He seemed to dwell too much on the past or on things he could do nothing about. She was probably better off without him. And then she just did not think about him much, or no more than she thought about other past relationships. Instead, she planned some future vacation trips as well as some activities with her friends.

Trista manifested features of a dismissive attachment style. Her independent pursuits, interests, and accomplishments were very important to her. Her relationships seemed to have a place in her independent lifestyle insofar as they helped her to be more "well rounded" or to have someone with whom she could engage in her interests and activities. She had little interest in emotional communications or relying on Anthony for any emotional support. She saw value in her partner's providing her with practical ideas or support, but since she devalued the emotional side of her life, she saw little value in sharing those aspects of her life with Anthony. If he shared those features of his life with her, she tended to listen politely but she often had a nagging fear that he might become dependent on her and she knew that she would not allow that. She had not decided that he was too dependent—it was just a worry—until he ended the relationship and then she concluded that he must have been all along.

While Blake had a preoccupied attachment style, Trista showed features of a dismissive style. Relationships were not seen as important enough for her to give them a high priority in her life, comparable with the priority she gave to her independent interests and pursuits.

Strategies to Increase the Meaning of Relationships in Your Life

The following are some strategies you may find useful in increasing the meaning of relationships that you embark on and maintain. After considering them, take a few moments more to see if you can think of some others that fit your unique characteristics and situation.

Address Your Sense of Autonomy

Avoiding relationships. If you devalue and avoid relationships for the sake of maintaining your autonomy, you might ask yourself why you do so. The following questions come to mind. You might take paper and pen and write down your responses while you review them.

Have relationships caused you more pain than pleasure in the past? What do you think the reasons for this were? How did you respond? Were there exceptions and how did you respond to them?

Have you experienced many significant relationship losses in your life? If so, when, with whom, and why? How did you respond? Did you rely on other relationships to help you through the losses or did you go it alone?

Have you attempted relationships and found yourself becoming dependent in a way that you could not control and did not want? Why do you think you felt this way?

Do you often think your potential friend or partner is too dependent on you, causing you to feel trapped or suffocated?

Are you more comfortable with thoughts than with emotion and have you found that being in a relationship engenders more emotion than you want to deal with? Do relationships tend to create considerable shame, fear of loss, sense of self-doubt, despair, rage?

Have you had many relationship-related obligations in the past that made it difficult for you to pursue your own interests?

Do you consistently avoid conflicts in relationships?

Do you feel obligated to meet the wishes of your friend or partner? Do you resent these perceived obligations?

Do you find that relationships impose restrictions on routines and activities you find enjoyable?

Preventing avoidance. If your answers to the questions above give you a good understanding of why you tend to avoid relationships in order to preserve your sense of autonomy, you might now reflect on whether you want to address those reasons. Hopefully, from the information provided in this book you will be aware of the various ways you might address them. Your past relationships do not have to dictate your future relationships. In reflecting on your past relationships you might well create new meanings for the events that were painful and for the times that you felt suffocated or limited within a relationship. These new meanings might well provide you with ideas for future options in relationships so that they enhance your sense of autonomy rather than diminish it.

Focusing on your partner. Develop the habit of focusing on the interests and activities of your partner. Try to experience what your partner is attending to and doing as deeply as possible so that you have a fairly good sense of his or her experiences. If you are not used to devoting so much attention to another person's life, you may have to do it consciously and review your success. Over time, as you develop this habit, you are likely to notice that you begin to do it without thinking and your partner's experiences are beginning to take on as much meaning for you as your own have. Eventually your life together will have as much meaning for you as do the interests that reflect your autonomy.

Identifying pleasurable activities. Focus on what you have done independently to create relaxation, joy, pride, and meaning in your life. Reflect on what activities you might do with your partner that will also be the source of relaxation, joy, pride, and meaning.

Develop Mindfulness

A somewhat different strategy for balancing autonomy and relationships is employing mindfulness. Earlier I explored the nature of mindfulness and its role in the development of reflective functioning. As we learn more about mindfulness we realize that mindfulness practice benefits many areas of your functioning, including attaining a balance between autonomy and relatedness. This is supported by Steven Porges's polyvagal theory, in which he states that the neurological processes active in the social engagement system are the same as those that are central to mindfulness.[1] Applying mindfulness to ourselves and others within relationships is an aspect of what Dan Siegel calls "mindsight," a mental awareness of relationships whereby we move from *me* to *we*, that "enables us to see that we are each part of an interconnected flow, a wider whole."[2] There are a number of reasons why mindfulness is able to facilitate the balance.

First, mindfulness improves your reflective functioning, enabling you to go more deeply into your inner life and become more aware of what you think, feel, value, and wish for. This awareness strengthens your sense of autonomy while also helping you to be more aware of how to attain healthy relationships.

Second, mindfulness helps you stay in the here-and-now, seeing value in all of the components of your life, without giving undue priority to one of them. Also, relationships are more likely to flourish when those involved are deeply engaged in the here and now. Such engagement enables you to be sensitive to your friend's expressions, intentions, and wishes while being responsive to him or her in an attuned, reciprocal manner. You are less likely to let your mind wander or to multitask, which might well

---

1. S. Porges, *The polyvagal theory* (New York: W.W. Norton, 2011).
2. Siegel, *The developing mind*, p. 58.

suggest to your friend that both he or she and the relationship were not that important to you.

Third, mindfulness facilitates your ability to maintain healthy attachments, whether the attachments involve relationships, interests, habits, or your favorite restaurants. Mindfulness does not mean that you have a lack of attachments. Rather, it means that you do not cling to your attachments. Within mindfulness, you do not anxiously obsess about the possibility of losing a relationship, not attaining a goal, or no longer being able to pursue a given activity. You would be sad, or even grieve the loss, but you would not have reduced the meaning of your life by clinging to someone or something out of an illusion that you might control the future or the other person. Mindfulness, in the context of healthy relationships, reminds you that controlling the other — his or her mind, feelings, and actions — will not strengthen the relationship or bring to it greater satisfaction and joy.

Finally, the richness of your emotional, reflective, and interpersonal life is dependent on the development — with more complex organization and greater density of nerve circuits — of the various regions of your prefrontal cortex. Research indicates that this area of your brain is enhanced by healthy relationships characterized by secure attachments as well as by mindfulness. Thus there are two central paths to the maturation of this important region of your brain. The strengthening of one path may support the functioning of the other. Developing a habitual state of mindfulness is likely to improve the health of your relationships.

Keep an Eye on the Horizon

While mindfulness stresses the value of living fully in the here and now, there is also value in noticing the distant horizon from time to time. When you think of your life in the future, what do you hope will be its central characteristics? If you are not likely to attain all that you might like to, what are your highest priorities? Is it important to you to have a deep, long-lasting relationship with a partner and similar meaningful relationships with one or more friends or family members? If so, have you given thought to how you might maintain and strengthen the relationships that you have in order to achieve those goals?

When you think of the future, you might ponder what sort of balance you want when you integrate your relationships with your individual, and possibly solitary, pursuits. If your career (research scientist at a competitive university) or your interest (climbing the 40 highest mountains in the world) takes you away from home a great deal, how realistic is it to expect that you will have a deep relationship with a partner who does not share your career or interests? There may be potential partners who would be satisfied with your long hours, days, or weeks away from home, but their numbers may be few.

You're probably not planning on climbing numerous mountains and don't have a hectic 80-hour-a-week profession. Using the skills explored in this book and developing (if necessary) and putting into play an autonomous attachment style, you will want and learn to practice a life characterized by an ongoing sense of acceptance, contentment, and enthusiasm—a life that includes very special healthy relationships.

A Final Exercise

Buy yourself a blank notebook for keeping a journal and commit yourself to using it, making entries by following the outline shown below. Follow this outline or a similar one that might better suit your unique life. For each entry, record what is true on that date. Then record what you want to be true by the next date.

Today's date (first entry in the journal)

> *Your sense of autonomy.* List three interests or activities that are central to your sense of who you are. Then answer these questions:
>
> - What is the most satisfying thing about that interest/activity?
> - How long have you done it, and how did it become more important?

- How long did you spend engaged in it?
- How important is it to you that it remain in your life?
- How disappointed are you when you cannot do it or it fails?

Relationships. List the three most important relationships in your life. Then elaborate on each element shown below as it pertains to your relationship:

- What you do together
- The amount of time you spend together
- What you share, talk about
- What you most enjoy doing
- What you argue about or avoid addressing
- What you like most about this relationship

Making changes in autonomy. List three changes to your sense of autonomy that you would like to see recorded under the next date in the journal.

Making general changes. List three general changes in your relationships that you would like to see recorded under the next date in the journal.

Complete this list 1 month, 3 months, 1 year, 2 years, and 5 years after the date of your first entry.

Read all your entries. Review your answers and compare them with your answers from previous entries. Note if you are successful in moving toward your goals for developing and maintaining healthy relationships in your life. If the changes are not exactly what you had hoped for, be patient and view yourself with playfulness, acceptance, curiosity, and empathy. If you maintain that attitude in your relationship with yourself, you are likely to be more able to maintain a similar attitude in your relationships with others.

Index

In this index, *t* denotes table.

acceptance, 49, 50–51, 106
acceptance, in PACE, 61–66
achievement, 96–97, 130, 161–62, 171
addictions, 96
adults
    attachment patterns in children versus, 7, 8*t*
    nonparent relationships with, 34–35
    See also friends; parents; partners; strangers
affection, within parent-child relationships, 24
    See also love; passion
agency, sense of, 156
    See also achievement; the future
Ainsworth, M., 2
ambivalent attachment pattern, 13, 14–15
amygdala, 53, 60, 62, 93
anger
    conflicts and, 28, 148
    developing relationships and, 110–12
    gender roles and, 113–14
    nonverbal communication mismatched to, 121, 129–130
    within parent-child relationships, 26–27
    See also emotions
anterior cingulate cortex, 52, 55, 60, 62, 93

anxiety
    anger and, 111, 112
    developing relationships and, 107–8
    nonverbal communication mismatched to, 130
    parental obsessiveness and infant, 141–42
    strangers and, 4
    See also insecurity
apologies, 151–54
approach system, in brain-based parenting, 59
arguments. *See* conflicts; differences; disagreements; misunderstandings
assertiveness, 113–14, 126–29, 148, 149
assumptions, 124–29, 150, 158
    See also motives
attachment disorganization, 30, 33
attachment figures, xv, 2
    See also friends; parents; partners
attachment patterns
    characteristics of, 8–10
    malleability of, 34–35
    parent-child relationships and, 6–10, 8*t*, 15–17
    steps in changing, 18–19
attachment security, xv–xvi, 142, 159
    See also secure attachment pattern

attachment theory, xv, 2
  See also infant attachment
attention. *See* joint attention
attunement, 53, 55, 60
  See also intersubjectivity; synchronization
autism spectrum disorders, xii
autobiographical narratives
  curiosity within, 66
  definition of, xvi
  factors influencing one's, 22, 35, 102–3, 105–6
  the future of relationships within, 170–71
  importance of examining one's, 39–42
  judgment of feelings in, 115
  self-concept and, 23–24
  themes within, 24–35
  See also life inventory
autonomic nervous system, 46–47, 48, 93, 116
  See also specific structures
autonomous attachment pattern
  anger and, 27
  examples of, 16–17, 18
  overview of, 8, 19, 155
  tolerance of differences and, 29
autonomy, 155–172
  See also self-concept
avoidance, 113–14, 151, 167–69
  See also denial, of conflicts
avoidant attachment pattern, 13
awareness. *See* attunement; intersubjectivity; joint attention

babies. *See* infant attachment
Baylin, J., 58
behavior, 50, 51
  See also motives; nonverbal communication

blame, 147
  See also shame and guilt
Bowlby, J., 2
boys, 11
  See also gender differences; gender roles
the brain
  gender differences in, 60–61
  Healthy Mind Platter and, 73*t*–74*t*
  relationships and influence on, 51–52, 55
  resonance circuitry within, 52–53, 55–56
  See also autonomic nervous system; *specific structures and neurotransmitters*
Brain-Based Parenting (Hughes and Baylin), 58

caregivers, xv
  See also parents
Cast Away, xi
change
  attachment patterns and, 18–19
  through alternative meanings, 22, 35, 40, 43
child abuse and neglect, 33, 120–21
  See also domestic violence; traumatic events
child-reading system, in brain-based parenting, 59
children
  acceptance of inner life of, 64
  attachment patterns in adults versus, 7, 8*t*
  brain-based parenting and, 58–59
  evaluations of social skills in, 64
  need to control in, 111
  reciprocity of communication by, 120–21

See also infant attachment;
    parent-child relationships
cocaine, 96
comfort, within parent-child rela-
    tionship, 25–26
See also empathy; support
commitment, 97–98, 139–140
common purpose, 54, 55
communication
    conflict replaying and, 149
    of feelings, 116–17
    mastering effective, 119–140
    See also assertiveness; nonverbal
        communication; reciprocity
compassion. *See* empathy; empathy,
    in PACE; support
conflict resolution
    assertiveness as part of, 113–14
    commitment and, 139–140
    overview of, 141–154
    within parent-child relationships,
        27–28
    with partners, 28–29, 137–140
conflicts
    alternative meaning of, 146, 150,
        158
    commitment versus, 98
    communication despite, 134–140
    denial of, 148–49
    developing relationships and,
        112–14
    diminished intimacy and, 28–29
    gender roles and, 11
    importance of relationships ver-
        sus, 144, 146–47
    within parent-child relationships,
        26–27, 143–44
    replaying of, 149
    secure attachment pattern and,
        18
    single addressing of, 150–51

See also differences; disagree-
    ments; misunderstandings
Connecting Time (Healthy Mind
    Platter), 73*t*
control, need to
    autonomy of partner and, 160
    childhood loss and, 33
    insecurity and, 110–12
    unresolved attachment pattern
        and, 30
    See also autonomy; indepen-
        dence, reduction in
corpus callosum, 60
culture, 10
curiosity, in PACE, 62, 66–69

dance of attunement, 53, 54
    See also intersubjectivity; synchro-
        nization
defensiveness
    acceptance versus, 49
    autonomic nervous system and,
        47
    communication of experience as
        fact and, 133
    conflict resolution and, 147
    exercises about, 72
    reciprocity versus, 121
    reflection on and inhibition of,
        56–58
    social engagement system and, 48
denial, of conflicts, 145–46, 148–49
    See also avoidance
The Developing Mind (Siegel), 51
developing relationships, 107–14,
    156–167
    See also relationships
differences
    conflict denial and, 148
    developing relationships and,
        109, 112–14

differences (*continued*)
　in emotional expressions, 25
　parent-child relationships and ex-
　　pression of, 29
　partners and tolerance of, 29–30
　See also conflicts; disagreements;
　　misunderstandings
disagreements, 88–89
　See also conflicts; differences;
　　misunderstandings
disappointments, within parent-
　child relationships, 25
discipline, within parent-child rela-
　tionships, 30
dismissive attachment pattern
　anger and, 27
　boys and, 11
　conflict denial and, 149
　examples of, 13, 15, 166–67
　lack of support and, 31
　overview of, 9, 19, 20
　traumatic events and, 33
distress, within parent-child relation-
　ships, 25–26, 143–44
　See also interactive repair
domestic violence, 111–12
　See also child abuse and neglect
dopamine, 53, 59, 61, 96
dorsolateral prefrontal cortex, 56, 62
Down Time (Healthy Mind Platter),
　74*t*

emotional competence, 114–18
emotional expressions, 24–26, 121,
　129–130
　See also facial expressions
emotional functioning, 75–76,
　92–93
emotions
　developing relationships and con-
　　flicting, 108–10

intersubjectivity and, 55
　within parent-child relationships,
　　24, 25
　reasoning and logic versus, 93–
　　94
　reflection on the past and influ-
　　ence of, 43–44
　relationships and influence of, 92
　relationships and negative, 100–
　　107, 110–12, 118
　relationships and positive, 94–
　　100, 117–18
　resonance circuitry and, 52, 53
　See also anger; feelings; *specific
　　emotions*
empathy, 53, 60
　See also support
empathy, in PACE, 62, 69–71
engagement. *See* social engagement
　system
enjoyment
　evaluations and, 49
　healthy relationships and, 96–97
　intersubjectivity and, 54
　playfulness and, 62–63
　See also love; pleasure
estrogen and estrogen receptors, 60,
　95
evaluations
　acceptance and, 49–50, 64
　developing relationships and, 108
　of inner life, 66
　praise and, 50–51
　See also judgments
excuses, 101, 103, 151, 152, 154
executive system, in brain-based par-
　enting, 59
experiences, communication of feel-
　ings versus, 132–33
exploration, infant attachment and,
　4–6

facial expressions
    communication of acceptance
        with, 49
    oxytocin and, 60
    playfulness and, 62
    reciprocity in communication
        and, 120, 121–22
    social engagement system and,
        47–48
    See also emotional expressions
facts, separating experiences from,
    132–33
failures, within parent-child rela-
    tionship, 25
    See also interactive repair
Family Futures, xii
feelings, 115–18, 120–24, 132–33
    See also emotions
fight or flight response. See auto-
    nomic nervous system
Focus Time (Healthy Mind Platter),
    73t
friends
    anger and relationship with, 27
    assumptions about, 125, 126–27
    autobiographical narratives and
        relationships with, 23
    brain-based parenting system and,
        59
    emotional expressions and rela-
        tionship with, 24, 26
    empathy for, 69
    negative emotions with, 103
    positive emotions with, 95, 99
    reciprocity between, 52
    See also partners
friendships, reflections on, 76
the future, 161, 170–71

gender differences, 60–61
gender roles, 10–11, 113–14

gestures and movements, 48–49, 62,
    120
    See also nonverbal communication
girls, 11
    See also gender differences; gen-
        der roles
gratitude, 99
guilt. See shame and guilt
gut sense, 93, 116
    See also emotional functioning

Hanks, T., xi
Healthy Mind Platter (Siegel and
    Rock), 73t–74t
hippocampus, 53, 60, 62, 93
hobbies. See interests and activities
Hughes, D., xii, 58

immobilization circuit, 47
immune system, 95
independence, reduction in, 110,
    149
    See also autonomy; control, need
        to
infant attachment
    caregivers and, xv
    interactive repair in, 141–42
    PACE and, 61, 62, 63–64
    parents and, 3–7, 53
    reciprocity of communication in,
        120
    See also parent-child relationships
infant distress, 3
    See also interactive repair
inner life
    acceptance of, 64, 65
    empathy and, 69
    evaluations of, 66
    management of feelings and, 117
    reciprocity in communication
        and, 121–22

inner working model, 7
　See also attachment patterns
insecurity
　conflicts and, 148, 149
　developing relationships and,
　　107, 108–9, 163
　enjoyment imbalance and, 97
　infant attachment and, 6
　mindfulness and, 170
　need to control and, 110–12
　relationship strength and, 106
　See also preoccupied attachment
　　pattern
insula, 53, 62, 93
interactive repair, 141–42
interests and activities, 159–160,
　162–63, 168–69, 171–72
interpersonal neurobiology, 51–61
　See also the brain; *specific struc-*
　　tures and neurotransmitters
intersubjectivity, 54–55
　See also attunement
intimacy, 28–29, 31–32, 55, 155–
　172
　See also affection, within parent-
　　child relationships

joint attention, 54
journaling, 161–64, 171–72
　See also autobiographical narra-
　　tives
judgments, 50, 115
　See also evaluations

life inventory, 161–62
　See also autobiographical narra-
　　tives
limit-setting. See discipline, within
　　parent-child relationships
listening. See communication; reci-
　　procity

loss, 32–33, 105–7
love
　healthy relationships and, 95
　loss and influence on, 105
　within parent-child relationships,
　　24
　reciprocity and, 99–100
　See also enjoyment; pleasure
lying, 102
　See also excuses

meaning-making, in relationships,
　159–160, 167–171
meaning-making system, in brain-
　based parenting, 59
meanings, alternative
　autobiographical narratives and,
　　39–40, 41–42
　change through, 22, 35, 40, 43
　of conflicts, 146
　the past as influencing the present
　　and, 35
　See also motives
memory, social, 60
me to *we*, 52, 169
　See also interpersonal neurobiol-
　　ogy
the mind, 51, 92
mindfulness, 169–170
　See also reflective functioning
mindsight, 169
mirror neurons, xi–xii, 52, 62
　See also attunement; synchroniza-
　　tion
miscommunication. See misunder-
　　standings
mistakes, apologies and, 151–54
misunderstandings, 124–29
　See also assumptions; conflicts;
　　differences; disagreements
mobilization circuit, 47

motives
  for avoiding relationships, 167–69
  in communication of feelings,
    116–17
  conflicts and, 148–49, 150, 158
  developing relationships and perception of, 109
  See also meanings, alternative
movements. *See* gestures and movements
multitasking, 60

negative emotions. *See* anger; emotions
neurobiology. *See* the brain; interpersonal neurobiology
neurotransmitters, 53, 59, 95
  See also specific neurotransmitters
nonparental relationships, 34–35
  See also adults; friends; partners
nonverbal communication
  assumptions and ignorance of,
    125–26
  congruence between verbal and,
    129–132
  inner life and, 121–22
  reciprocity in, 120
  social engagement system and,
    47–49
  synchronization and, 53
  See also emotional expressions; facial expressions; gestures and movements; voice
nucleus accumbens, 93

opinions. *See* differences
oxytocin, 53, 59, 60, 95

PACE (playfulness, acceptance, curiosity, and empathy), 61–73

pain. *See* loss
parental withdrawal, 28
parent-child relationships
  attachment patterns and, 15–17
  autobiographical narratives and,
    23
  distress within, 25–26, 144
  interactive repair within, 141–42
  reciprocity in, 120–21
  themes within, 24–35, 44–45
  See also children; infant attachment; parents
parenting, brain-based, 58–59
  See also parent-child relationships
parents
  infant attachment and, 3–7, 53
  interactive repair by, 141–42
  reciprocity of communication by,
    120
  world view and influence of, 5–6
  See also caregivers; parent-child relationships
partners
  assertiveness with, 113–14
  assumptions about, 125–26, 127–29
  brain-based parenting system and,
    59
  communication of feelings to,
    116–17
  conflict resolution with, 28–29,
    137–140
  discipline's influence on relationships with, 30–31
  emotional expressions with,
    24–26
  misperception of motives of, 109,
    158
  need to control, 160
  negative emotions with, 102,
    103–4

partners (*continued*)
  positive emotions with, 96, 98, 99
  prevention of avoidance of rela-
    tionship with, 168–69
  reality in relationship with, 109–
    10
  reciprocity between, 52, 53
  synchronization between long-
    time, 53–54
  tolerance of differences by, 29–30
  See also friends
passion, 98, 149
the past, 35, 43–44, 161
  See also autobiographical narra-
    tives
peers. *See* friends
Physical Time (Healthy Mind Platter), 73t
playfulness, in PACE, 61, 62–63
Play Time (Healthy Mind Platter),
  73t
pleasure
  attunement and, 55
  brain-based parenting and, 59
  dopamine and, 53, 58
  playfulness and, 61, 62
  See also enjoyment; love
polyvagal theory, 169
Porges, S., 47, 61, 169
positive emotions. *See* emotions;
  specific emotions
praise, 50–51
prefrontal cortex, 52, 55, 62, 170
preoccupied attachment pattern
  anger and, 27
  conflict replaying and, 149
  examples of, 13, 160
  girls and, 11
  overview of, 9, 20, 21
  strategies for mitigating, 160–64
  support quality and, 31

traumatic events and, 33
  See also insecurity
the present, 35, 161
  See also attunement; intersubjec-
    tivity; mindfulness
prolactin, 95
purpose. *See* common purpose;
  meaning-making, in relationships; meanings, alternative;
  motives

reality, developing relationships and,
  109–10
reasoning and logic, 93–94
  See also reflective functioning
reciprocity
  in communication of feelings,
    120–24
  enjoyment in relationships and,
    96, 97
  love and, 99–100
  in relationships with partners, 52,
    53
  See also communication
reflection
  acceptance and, 64
  on defensiveness, 56–58
  emotional influences upon,
    43–44
  empathy and curiosity in, 62
  parent-child relationship themes
    and, 44–45
  relationships and moment-to-mo-
    ment, 55–58, 82–89
  on shame, 104
reflective functioning, 75–90, 92–
  93, 117
  See also mindfulness
relationship detachment, 31–32
relationships
  the brain and influence of, 51–52

conflict versus importance of, 144, 146–47
developing, 107–14, 156–167
influence of self-concept on, xv, xvi
meaning-making in, 159–160, 167–171
moment-to-moment reflections on, 55–58, 82–89
reflecting on general, 76–80
reflecting on specific, 80–82, 89–90
reflective versus emotional functioning in, 92–93
See also friends; parent-child relationships; partners
religion, 10
resonance circuitry, 52–53, 55–56
reward system, in brain-based parenting, 59

safety
    acceptance and, 64
    autonomic nervous system and, 47, 48
    infant attachment and, 3–4
    through playfulness, 62, 63
    See also defensiveness
Schore, A., 51
secure attachment pattern, 18, 159
    See also attachment security
security. See infant attachment; safety
self-concept
    attachment figures and, 2
    autobiographical narratives and, 23–24
    awareness of feelings and, 115–16
    expression of differences and, 29
    relationships and influence of, xv, xvi
    See also autonomy

self-doubts, developing relationships and, 109
    See also anxiety; insecurity
sensory input, 48
shame and guilt
    anger and, 27
    avoidance of apology and, 151
    discipline and, 30
    healthy relationships and, 101–4
    parental withdrawal and, 28
    See also blame
Siegel, D., 51, 52, 169
significant others. See friends; partners
Sleep Time (Healthy Mind Platter), 74t
social engagement system, 47–51, 61–71, 169
spouses. See partners
Stern, D., 120
strangers, 4
substance abuse, 96
support, 25–26, 31–32
    See also empathy
survival, 3
synchronization
    brain-based parenting and, 59
    between long-time partners, 53–54
    social engagement system and, 48–49
    See also attunement; mirror neurons; resonance circuitry

talking. See communication; reciprocity
temporal lobes, 62
testosterone receptors, 60
thalamus, 53
threat, 50
    See also autonomic nervous system; defensiveness

Time In (Healthy Mind Platter),
        73t
toddlers. *See* children; infant attach-
        ment
traumatic events, 33–34
    See also child abuse and neglect;
        domestic violence

unresolved attachment pattern,
        9–10, 20, 21, 30

vasopressin, 95
voice, 47–48, 49, 62, 120
vulnerabilities, 25–26, 112
        See also anxiety; insecurity

will power, 93
        See also reflective functioning
"Wilson" (*Cast Away*), xi
world view, parental influence
        upon, 5–6